My Encounter with the
BIG CAT
and Other Adventures
in Ranthambhore

My Encounter with the
BIG CAT
and Other Adventures
in Ranthambhore

Daulat Singh Shaktawat

NIYOGI
BOOKS

Published by
NIYOGI BOOKS
Block D, Building No. 77,
Okhla Industrial Area, Phase-I,
New Delhi-110 020, INDIA
Tel: 91-11-26816301, 26818960
Email: niyogibooks@gmail.com
Website: www.niyogibooksindia.com

Text ©: Daulat Singh Shaktawat
Editorial and Design: Write Media

ISBN: 978-93-86906-14-4
Year of Publication: 2018

Printed at: Niyogi Offset Pvt. Ltd., New Delhi, India

CONTENTS

Ranthambhore Tiger Reserve

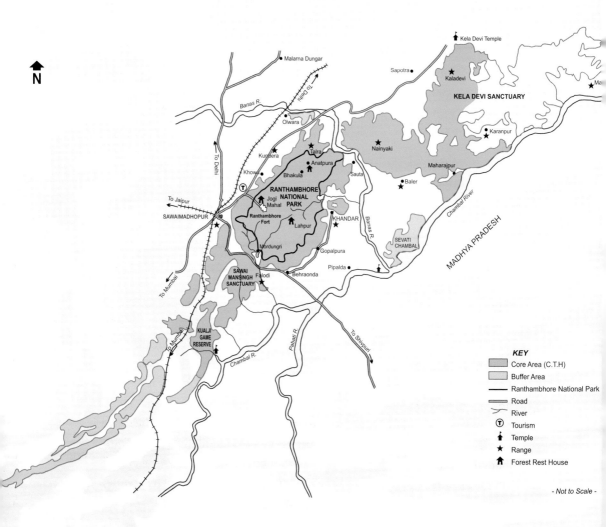

KEY

- Core Area (C.T.H)
- Buffer Area
- Ranthambhore National Park
- Road
- River
- Ⓣ Tourism
- Temple
- ★ Range
- Forest Rest House

- Not to Scale -

AUTHOR'S NOTE

*I*t was a hot summer afternoon in May 2010. My friend, Akhil Chandra, a committed wildlife enthusiast and photographer, was visiting me at the Ranthambhore Tiger Reserve and we were engrossed in an animated discussion. I was describing in great detail my last encounter with a tiger, when a field staff member informed me that tigress T-13, along with her two young cubs, had killed a blue bull in the Sohan Kutch area the previous night. She was still with the bull, which she had dragged into a nearby thicket.

In spite of having spent over three decades in the forests, any opportunity to observe a tiger still excites me. Akhil was equally elated to hear the news so we decided to rush to the site of the kill to photograph the mother with her cubs. As it was a long drive, we continued our discussion. I told Akhil about the advice of my gurus, Kailash Sankhala and Fateh Singh Rathore, to observe all the sightings in the jungle and to carefully record them in a diary. I had been following this routine diligently and now had a treasure trove of memories. I give him a diary that was in my camera bag.

By the time we reached Sohan Kutch it was 2.30 pm. The heat of the afternoon, coupled with the hot summer winds, had probably pushed the tiger family to a nearby rock cave. We decided to wait and parked under the shade of a tree. Meanwhile, Akhil was flipping through my diary. He was absolutely amazed at the wealth of experiences and incidents recorded. Accompanied by photographs, the diary was a mine of information about animal behaviour.

'Why don't you put all this together in a book?' he asked. 'I'll help you with it, if you so desire.'

There, on that hot May afternoon, deep inside the Ranthambhore forest, was planted the 'seed' of this book.

We managed to see T-13 and her cubs a little later. We took photographs and sat watching their antics for some time. Akhil's suggestion was playing at the back of my mind. As time passed, my diaries kept getting bulkier and I started thinking seriously about putting my experiences together in a book. I discussed this with my wife who said it was a great idea and encouraged me to get on with it. But, due to my pre-occupation with work in the field, as well as the fact that I was often posted at the headquarters, I could not get down to pursue that dream. Then, calamity struck! My near-death experience on 20 August 2010 made me realise the transient nature of things.

Being blessed with a new lease of life, I decided, from now onwards, I would do only what my heart desired.

My treatment went on for over two-and-a-half years. The tender care and nursing of my wife, Om Kanwar; my sons, Satybhan and Shivbhan; daughters, Monika and Suman; daughter-in-law, Rekha and my little angel, my granddaughter Vanshika, Khyati and Rohitashva Rathore encouraged me to recover and get back on my feet soon. I went back to Ranthambhore to work once again with the wild denizens that I have always loved.

I started putting together my field notes for a book. Shivbhan and Monika helped me give some semblance to my documentation and translated my handwritten notes. They are both working and have busy lives, yet they took the time to help me put it all together. I am indebted to Dr Subhadeep Bhattacharjee who was instrumental in collating all the data and organising it as well. Once the basic script was ready, Sangita and Akhil Chandra helped re-write the incidents in a more readable way. Akhil then put me in touch with Bikash Niyogi of Niyogi Books for bringing my dream to fruition.

During my postings at Ranthambhore there have been many exhilarating and incredible incidents and it was difficult to choose which one to write about first. Other than the most devastating experience of my life, I have narrated my encounters with Ustad and the joy of watching tiger cubs grow to adulthood.

I hope that, soon, I will be able to bring to the reader other such encounters in the wild.

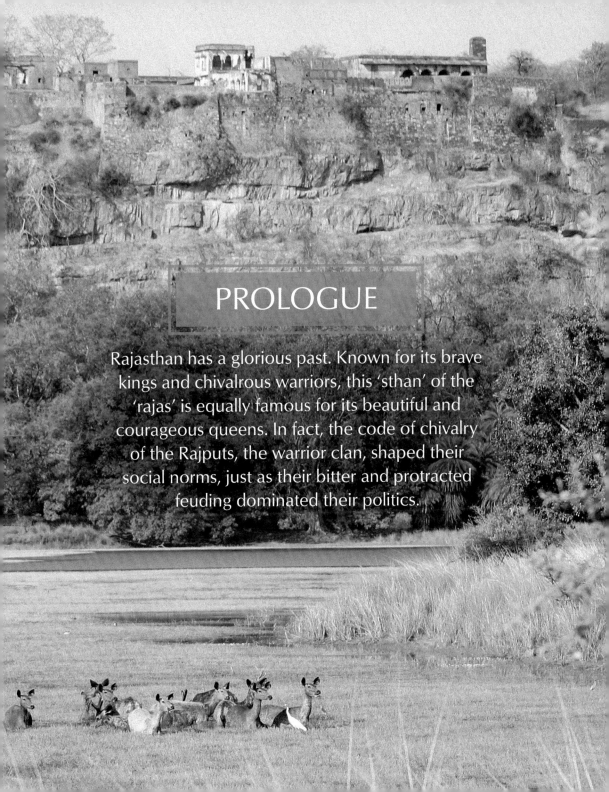

PROLOGUE

Rajasthan has a glorious past. Known for its brave kings and chivalrous warriors, this 'sthan' of the 'rajas' is equally famous for its beautiful and courageous queens. In fact, the code of chivalry of the Rajputs, the warrior clan, shaped their social norms, just as their bitter and protracted feuding dominated their politics.

*T*he vibrant costumes of the people provide a stark contrast and much-needed colour to this desert state of India. The other relief to the landscape is provided by the surprisingly rich fauna and the unique desert flora, mostly confined to the east of the Aravalli hill ranges. The Sawai Madhopur district, located on the eastern edge of Rajasthan, is home to the Ranthambhore Tiger Reserve, which is 160 km from Jaipur, the state capital. Sawai Madhopur is a small, ubiquitous Rajasthani town that owes its celebrity status to the Ranthambhore Tiger Reserve and the Tri-Netra Ganesh Temple inside the Ranthambhore Fort, a UNESCO World Heritage site. The history of Sawai Madhopur revolves around this majestic fort, its inaccessible

MD PARASHAR

*The Tri-Netra Ganesh Temple, which is situated inside
the Ranthambhore Fort*

There are many ruins
scattered all over the
Ranthambhore Tiger
Reserve. Here, a tigress
(T-18) is resting under
an ancient chhatri

DAULAT SINGH SHAKTAWAT

ramparts and courageous occupants. Even today, the ruins of the great domes and *chhatris* (canopies), along with the Ganesh Temple, tell stories of a magnificent past.

However, Sawai Madhopur is now synonymous with the Ranthambhore Tiger Reserve, known worldwide for its tigers and other fauna. Ranthambhore was established as the Sawai Madhopur Game Sanctuary in 1955 and was declared as one of the Project Tiger Reserves in 1973. The central part of the Sawai Madhopur Sanctuary became Ranthambhore National Park in 1980. In 1984, the adjacent forests of Sawai Man Singh and Keladevi were declared as sanctuaries and, subsequently, in 1991, they were annexed to the Tiger Reserve.

Situated at the confluence of the two mountain ranges, the Aravallis and the Vindhayas, the terrain of Ranthambhore is mostly undulating with dry deciduous forests and tropical scrub vegetation. While the plateaus have sparse vegetation, the valleys are green with dense jamun groves. The most dominant tree species found in this region is dhonk, along with associated species such as dhak, khair, ber, tendu and salar. The perennial water streams (*nallah*s), lakes or *talav*s such as Padam, Rajbagh, Mallik, Gilai Sagar and Man Sarovar are a major

T-18 patrolling the Padam talav area. While the plateaus have sparse vegetation, the valleys are green with dense jamun groves

DAULAT SINGH SHAKTAWAT

DAULAT SINGH SHAKTAWAT

Situated at the confluence of two mountain ranges, the terrain of Ranthambhore is mostly undulating. A view of the Indala plateau in the Lahapur area after the monsoon season

Flycatchers feeding their chicks. Ranthambhore's faunal bounty includes a large variety of migratory birds, along with around 250 to 300 resident species

source of water in the Tiger Reserve. There are many ruins of old walls, *chhatri*s, mosques and stepwells (*bawdi*s) scattered all over the Reserve. These add to the beauty of the place and often a tiger or a leopard can be seen reposing in the shade of these ruins. Tigers and leopards are the main predators in Ranthambhore. The lesser predators are the jungle

DAULAT SINGH SHAKTAWAT

Clockwise from top left: Wild boars near the Mallik anicut; a male spurfowl with chicks; a view of the Mallik talav with crocodiles and painted storks; an Indian rock python predates on a chinkara

An albino spotted deer with a herd. In addition to prey species, Ranthambhore's biodiversity includes hyenas, jackals, civets, ratels and porcupines

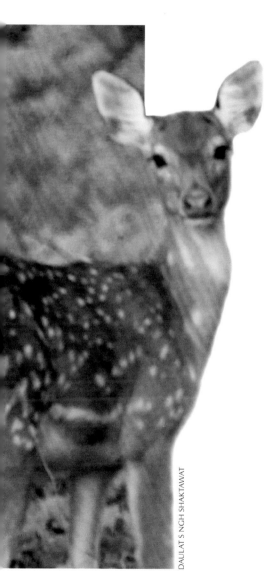

DAULAT SINGH SHAKTAWAT

cat, desert cat, caracal and the rusty spotted cat. Sloth bears also inhabit the rugged terrain but are not often sighted. Sambar, chital, chinkara and nilgai are found in abundance here. In addition to these prey species, Ranthambhore's biodiversity includes hyenas, jackals, civets, ratels and porcupines. Crocodiles can be seen in the lakes or basking on the banks. The faunal bounty also includes a large variety of migratory birds, along with 250 to 300 resident species.

Any commentary or experience with the magnificent national animal of the country would be incomplete without first talking about the international obsession for the big cat and Project Tiger. To halt the rapid decline of the tiger population in the country and to save it from extinction, the Government of India, under the leadership of the then Prime Minister, Indira Gandhi, launched one of the world's most ambitious conservation efforts, Project Tiger, in 1973. A major factor contributing to the decline of the tiger population in

Krishna (T-19) with her second litter. Tigers and leopards are the main predators in Ranthambhore. The lesser predators are the jungle cat, desert cat, caracal and the rusty spotted cat

*Sambhar running away from a
tiger attack at the Mallik* talav

India was population explosion, leading to habitat destruction. Forests
were felled ruthlessly all over the country to make way for agricultural
fields and factories, in addition to other developmental activities. Trophy
hunting by the Britishers armed with guns and the former Maharajas and
Nawabs accelerated the process of the decline of tigers and other wildlife
in India. The fate of the tiger was sealed by the turn of the century when
the demand for its body parts for oriental medicines reached a new high.
Poaching and the illegal export of tiger bones posed a serious threat to
the survival of this majestic cat in its natural habitat.

The Sawai Madhopur Junction of the West Central Railway pays a visual tribute to the mighty tiger.
This station has been renamed the Tiger City station

DAULAT SINGH SHAKTAWAT

Tigers and leopards
are the main predators
at the Ranthambhore
Reserve. Often a
leopard can be
sighted, looking out
for his kill

DAULAT SINGH SHAKTAWAT

Project Tiger's aim was to reverse the alarmingly low number of tigers, which had dipped to over 1,800 in the entire country. For this, the Project had to take over the monitoring of large areas of forests that were inhabited not only by the tiger but also by its prey species. The health of a forested area is dependent on the tiger, which is at the apex of the ecosystem, as well as on the smaller animals and the flora. To save the tiger, it is imperative to save the entire ecosystem of the region. The criteria for selecting the Reserves to launch this Project was that each site should be representative of a certain type of tiger habitat and the selected area should be as undisturbed as possible, with a healthy population of the prey species and the tiger.

In the first phase of Project Tiger in 1973, nine habitat types (Reserves) were selected across the country. Ranthambhore was the only habitat selected from the state of Rajasthan. From nine Tiger Reserves in 1973 under Project Tiger to 50 Tiger Reserves today, under the National Tiger Conservation Authority (NTCA), the tiger conservation programme has progressed well. In spite of some major hiccups along the way, with tiger numbers dipping down to a mere 1,000 plus, the Project is considered as one of the most successful conservation efforts in the world. The tiger population in India now stands at approximately 2,226.

TRACKING AND MONITORING THE TIGER

Tigers have always been tracked by the impression of their pugmarks on the soil. From ancient folklore to the experiences of Jim Corbett in Kumaon and other naturalists in the wild, a sure-shot way of reaching a tiger was to follow his pugmarks.

𝒯igers do not have similar pugmarks and a single pugmark can also vary in size and shape in different types of soils. This was a major tool in the past to count tigers in the wild during census operations. In 1966, Saroj Raj Chaudhary, Founder Director of Simlipal National Park in Odisha, introduced the method of pugmark monitoring to assess the tiger population. Considering that this was the only known method at that time, the technique was widely accepted and used for the next four decades. During the larger part of my service in the Forest Department, I have counted and identified tigers using this system.

Field staff members, such as the beat guards, were provided special training. They would leave the checkpost early in the morning with their pugmark tracking kit and walk along tiger trails, waterholes, ponds and other forest paths looking for fresh pugmarks. After coming across a distinct set of pugmarks, they would pour plaster of Paris (POP) in the impression on the ground. Information regarding the site from where the pugmark was recorded was etched by them on the reverse side of the POP impression. These plaster casts, along with field information, were dispatched to the range and division headquarters for further analysis with the aid of maps. Repetitions and overlaps of the same tiger or leopard were removed. The pattern of pugmarks also helped to identify whether it was a male, female or cub, before narrowing it down to a particular one.

In order to collect the perfect cast, the Ranthambhore Park authorities started preparing pugmark impression pads (PIPs) with 2 mm thick soil layers in areas frequently visited by tigers. This was felt necessary by the beat guards as, often, owing to the variation in soil types, such as sandy or moist clay, the pugmark of an individual tiger could differ

DAULAT SINGH SHAKTAWAT

*Making a plaster cast of a tiger pugmark, a major tool in the past
to count tigers in the wild during census operations*

considerably. The preparation and maintenance of the PIP resolved this issue. Nonetheless, the accuracy of pugmark monitoring relied heavily on the skills, judgement and honesty of the beat guards. There have been instances where, in spite of a decline in the tiger population, the forest staff has continued to show a healthy number of tigers.

Pugmark monitoring of tigers in Ranthambhore was in practice since its inception to the launch of Project Tiger in 1973. It worked quite well here and we managed to keep a tab on the tigers in the Reserve. During the late eighties, eminent wildlife scientist Dr K Ullas Karanth of the Wildlife Conservation Society (WCS) started working with camera traps to understand if the tiger population could be efficiently estimated using a 'Capture Recapture' framework. In 1995, he published a scientific article where he explained that the population of tigers, or any other naturally marked animal that could be individually identified, should be estimated using camera traps as the results obtained were extremely accurate.

The fluctuating and declining tiger numbers in India, along with uncertain records, prompted conservationists to criticise the pugmark method and adopt the new camera trap method which relied on technology rather than human psychology. Thereafter, this technique was taken up by Project Tiger and also by different state forest departments across the country. Camera traps are increasingly being used to study wildlife and to conduct population estimations.

A camera trap is a remotely activated camera that is equipped with a motion sensor or an infrared sensor. These cameras are set up in forests along trails or ravines, often in inaccessible areas. Whenever any animal

Camera trap photograph of a
male tiger (T-28)

or object goes in front of it, a picture is clicked automatically. It is an efficient method for preparing inventories and for population studies of the species as individual tigers can be recognised by their stripe markings. They are then given a unique ID number to manage them. All duplicate photographs of a particular animal can easily be sorted out and segregated. Thus, camera traps are important non-invasive tools for assessing numbers, patterns of activity and habitat use, all key elements for wildlife conservation.

This method was adopted in Ranthambhore for tiger census in 2006. From 2006 to 2010, grid areas of four square kilometres (2 km x 2 km) were sampled with one pair of cameras. In 2011-12, the National Tiger

Conservation Authority (NTCA) and the Wildlife Institute of India (WII) refined this method and more intensive sampling was done in revised grid areas of two square kilometres (1.43 km x 1.43 km). These camera traps were deployed in almost every corner of Ranthambhore except completely inaccessible areas such as steep cliffs, ravines and other human-dominated peripheral areas. In the peripheral and adjoining rural areas of Ranthambhore, village wildlife volunteers of the NGO Tiger Watch are actively working with camera traps and helping the forest staff by photo-capturing the tigers occupying these areas. The camera traps not only capture tigers but also other elusive mammals such as leopards, striped hyenas, caracals, jungle cats, desert cats, ratels, civets and so on.

In this book, I have used the numeric identity of tigers to describe their behaviour, location, territories and activities. This has been made possible only by the use of camera traps and stripe identification software. These ID numbers are used not only by forest guards but are also referred to by wildlife lovers who visit the Reserve often.

Another method in use for the last few decades to monitor tigers is radio telemetry. This technique had been employed all over the world on different animals but was first used for tigers by American scientists in Royal Chitwan National Park, Nepal, during the 1980s. It involves chemically immobilising the tiger by shooting a dart containing sedatives (a mixture of ketamine and xylazine). This is a highly skilled operation and can be undertaken only after determining the exact amount of the dose of sedatives to be given. The assessment is dependent on guessing accurately the body weight of the animal to be immobilised. Once the animal is sedated, its body is covered with a wet cloth to keep its

*Clockwise from top left: Camera trap photographs of a
porcupine; a mother sloth bear with sub-adult cubs; a caracal;
a ratel; leopards; a hyena*

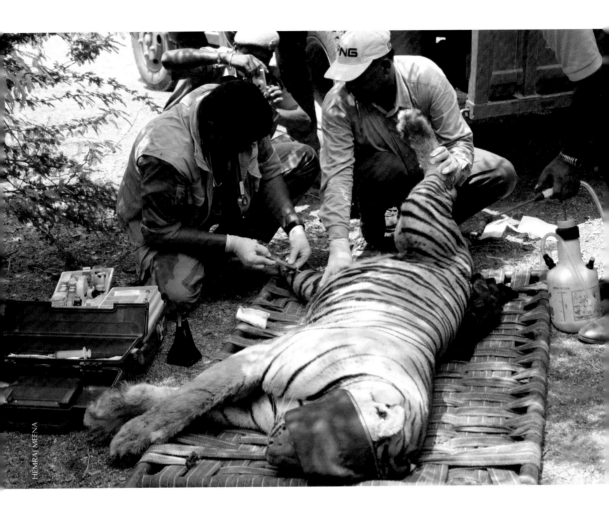

*The author with Dr Parag Nigam. They are taking the blood
sample of a tranquillised tigress (T-44) before its translocation to
the Sariska Tiger Reserve*

temperature normal and blood pressure in check. Scientists quickly weigh the animal, take physical measurements, collect blood and hair samples and finally fit a radio collar around the neck. The animal is then revived by administering an antidote and allowed to go its way.

The radio collar emits signals that are received by a dedicated receiver with the help of an antenna, within a given radius. Field staff members are equipped with this receiver and antenna to monitor the movements of the radio-collared animal. Some tigers have been chemically immobilised and radio-collared in Ranthambhore to monitor their movements and behaviour patterns. Chemical immobilisation is also used to treat sick or injured animals. Having received training from the Wildlife Institute of India, Dehradun, in 1987, I now use this technique during emergency situations to immobilise big cats and other carnivores and herbivores for their treatment and management-related activities.

MY NEAR-DEATH EXPERIENCE

Friday, 20 August 2010. I can never forget that day, which was undoubtedly the darkest day of my life. It was the day I nearly died.

$\mathcal{I}$ woke up early as usual and started my routine of getting ready to go into the jungle for patrolling. I was just about to move out when, at 6 am, I got a wireless message from RS Shekhawat, Deputy Director, Ranthambhore Tiger Reserve. A male tiger had crossed the Reserve boundary and had entered a village, Bhuri Pahari, near the periphery. He had killed a buffalo and was now hiding in the crop fields bordering the village. I had to get there to take stock of the situation and to try and push the tiger back into the Reserve.

As I had handled such situations earlier, I could well imagine the scene in Bhuri Pahari. I picked up a tranquillising gun and other equipment and got ready to leave, along with three forest staff members. I also called up the local veterinarian, Dr Rajeev Garg, to accompany me. Driving along the 40 km distance, I could not help but dwell on the man-wild animal conflict that is increasing at alarming proportions across the globe but more particularly in densely populated India. Deforestation and the loss of habitat of wild animals bring them in direct confrontation with villages overlapping or bordering natural wildlife territories. Crop damage, livestock depredation, injuries and a loss of human lives are all sensitive issues that need to be handled with care and foresight.

DAULAT SINGH SHAKTAWAT

T-7 (seen on previous page with his sibling, T-6), on a blue bull kill. T-7 is the tiger who attacked the author

T-7: Deforestation and the loss of habitat of wild animals bring them in direct confrontation with villages overlapping or bordering natural wildlife territories

DAULAT SINGH SHAKTAWAT

We reached Bhuri Pahari at 8:30 am and were totally taken aback by what we saw there. A large number of villagers had surrounded an agricultural field with four to five feet high crops. About 60 to 70 forest staff members, with an equal number of police personnel, were trying to control the angry, slogan shouting, stone throwing mob. I realised immediately that it was going to be impossible to flush the tiger out and make him move towards the Reserve. Yet, we had to do something proactive to de-escalate the situation. So, we decided to track the tiger amid the shoulder-high crops. It took a while but we managed to locate him. The tiger was

HEMRAJ MEENA

hiding near a mud mount and some villagers perched on tree branches could also see him. But, as we were standing on the crop field, he was not clearly visible. The Deputy Director, who had also arrived by then, requested the police personnel to control the swelling crowd and tell them to stay at a safe distance so that the tiger could get free passage to the forest, a mere two kilometres away. This infuriated the crowd further and they began throwing stones in the direction of the tiger. People from neighbouring villages had also started gathering there and the mob was absolutely unmanageable.

A large number of villagers had surrounded an agricultural field with four to five feet high crops at Bhuri Pahari

Deputy Director Shekhawat, forester Hukum Chand, forest guard Rajveer and I now moved to the opposite side of the mud mount, in an attempt to get a clear view of the tiger. We lit some firecrackers and threw them in the direction of the tiger, hoping that he would get scared and move towards the forest. After we did this a couple of times, the tiger got up, roared and ran towards the neighbouring field. But the noise from the crowd was even louder than the fireworks, and the tiger settled down again among the crops. It was now totally impossible to reach the tiger in order to tranquillise him. We could not drive our Gypsy into the crop

HEMRAJ MEENA

field because, along with zero visibility, there were deep ravines as well. Therefore, we decided to move away with all our tranquillising equipment and come back later, when the crowd had thinned.

As we were in the process of doing so, I got a message from the Assistant Conservator of Forests (ACF), SR Yadav, that the crowd on the other side was creating a riot. They were threatening the police force that if the tiger was not captured or killed immediately, they would forcefully grab their guns and kill the tiger themselves. I was advised to reach the spot

People from neighbouring villages had also started gathering there and the mob was absolutely unmanageable

immediately with my team and somehow go ahead with the operation. I had a foreboding sense of disaster as I moved ahead on foot with the three forest staff members into the crop field. I loaded the tranquillising gun, locked it and handed it over to Hukum Chand while I updated ACF Yadav about our position on the wireless. Suddenly, about eight to ten villagers came out of the ravines and started manhandling me and my team. They grabbed the gun from Hukum Chand and shouted that they were capable of shooting the tiger themselves. They had no idea how to handle the gun, which was loaded with a mixture (7 ml) of ketamine and xylazine. Even 2 ml of this deadly medicine can kill a human. I was worried that the sensitive safety catch of the gun may open; the slightest pressure could trigger the medicine. More men came in from the ravine and joined this inebriated lot. I tried to reason with them and get the gun back. We were standing amid ravines while the rest of the crowd, the police force and forest staff were at the opposite side of the ravines, about half a kilometre away. They could see the confusion and the manhandling happening here. Thankfully, nature guide Hemraj Meena and a few local residents managed to control the rowdy assaulters.

My years of experience told me that the tiger could not be tranquillised in this situation as he was not even visible among the dense crops. Moreover, the field was surrounded on all sides by a sea of unruly spectators. ACF Yadav and I tried to convince the crowd to disperse to enable us to do our work. This infuriated them even more so I took the gun and started walking among the tall crops in search of the tiger, along with the team. After nearly an hour of combing the field, we managed to see a hint of yellow-and-black stripes. Against my better judgment, I fired the dart in that direction. It seemed to hit the tiger. But, for the sedative to take effect

*The author (second from left) with the team from the
Ranthambhore Tiger Reserve looking for the tiger amid tall crops*

on the tiger, silence was required. The situation was far from quiet as the crowd continued shouting. When we requested the mob to stay calm, they pelted stones towards the tiger who stood up and started running towards the jungle with a roar. After covering a distance of almost half a kilometre, he once again settled down among the crops. Dr Garg and I went to inspect the place where the tiger had been crouching when the dart was shot. We found the dart with a twisted needle. There was blood and some tiger hair on the needle. The dart had definitely hit him, but probably on the bone and, therefore, the medicine may not have been released properly.

The situation was getting worse and more dangerous. We had a furious, cornered tiger hiding in the crop field surrounded by an equally angry crowd. I had no other option but to locate the tiger once again, against all odds. Accompanied by Hukum Chand, Rajveer and Tulsiram, I went into the field to look for the tiger. There was almost zero visibility as we moved around. Then we saw a big mud mount surrounded by thick bushes, nearly 50 metres away from us. I realised that this mount could well provide us with a vantage point to look for the tiger. With a lot of difficulties, slipping a couple of times, we managed to climb the muddy mount. People sitting on treetops could apparently see the tiger and they pointed in his direction. I could only get a faint glimpse of tiger stripes, about 50 to 60 feet away. The other three foresters were behind me and we could not figure out the position or the posture of the tiger.

HEMRAJ MEENA

People sitting on treetops, in search of the tiger. The crowd was increasing and the angry mob was getting difficult to control

The tiger, however, could see us standing on the mud mount clearly. He snarled at us, then turned and started moving in the opposite direction from us, towards the forest. We waited to get a glimpse of him moving away. Suddenly, we heard a roar from very near. Before I could react, I saw the tiger emerging from dense cover in front of me, barely eight to ten feet away. He was snarling and appeared extremely aggressive. I had the tranquillising gun in my right hand but, before I could think of doing anything, the tiger had already pounced on me.

I screamed and tried to turn away, but it was too late! The tiger was on me, inserting his claws into my body, my right hand clenched between his jaws. His right paw was on my chest, claws digging in. I amassed all my strength and tried to push him away but I fell down on the ground with the massive weight of the tiger on top of me. It was the worst nightmare of my lifetime, only this time it was for real. I could hear and feel my bones being crushed and cracked, from my forehead to the right side of my face and jaw. I could barely breathe and started preparing myself for death. Then, suddenly, the weight was lifted and the tiger was gone with a roar. I was still alive! I just could not believe it. Somehow, I managed to stand up and look for help. There was no one around.

The author leads the
operation in the fields
where the tiger had
managed to hide in
the dense cover

SUNNY PATIL

SUNNY PATIL

*The tiger is spotted in the forest and the
team heads towards him*

The author is attacked by the tiger; his hand is in the tiger's jaws

The author amasses all his strength and tries to push the tiger away. He falls down on the ground, with the massive weight of the tiger on top of him

SUNNY PATIL

SUNNY PATIL

DR DHARMENDRA KHANDAL

Colleagues try to stop the bleeding from the author's face
by wrapping it with cloth

I thought to myself that I could not have survived this horrific incident to be now abandoned by all. It was taking a lot of effort on my part just to stand up. I touched my face and found a ball-like something hanging next to my right cheek. It was my eye, which had come out of the ocular socket. There was blood everywhere. Yet, surprisingly, I could not feel any pain. Then I was overtaken by anger and a rage so violent that I started

DR DHARMENDRA KHANDAL

*A charpai (bed) is used as a makeshift stretcher
to carry the author*

shaking. This anger was against the shouting, unruly and crazy mob that
had infuriated the cornered tiger so much that he had mauled me. It was
also directed at my staff members who were not around when I needed
them the most. I shouted at my helplessness till my lungs seemed to burst.
This made some people come running towards me, they were amazed
that I was still alive for they had given me up for dead.

Then the pain started. An intolerable, throbbing agony, the kind I had not experienced ever before. Hemraj and my staff wrapped a towel around my face to control the bleeding. I could hear Deputy Director Shekhawat's and ACF Yadav's voices in the backdrop, arranging for me to be put on a cot and then in a Gypsy. I was conscious enough to tell them that my blood group was A+ and that they should arrange

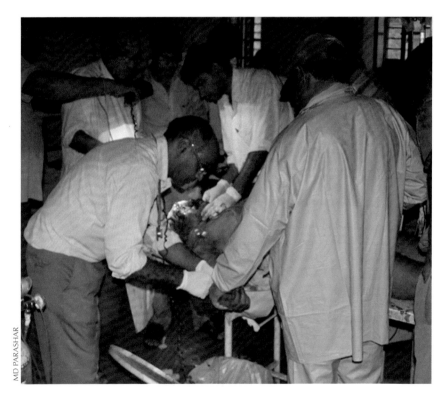

*First aid being administered to the author after the
horrific attack*

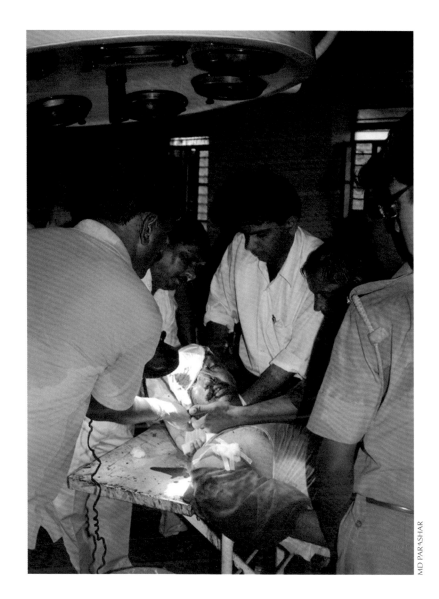

MD PARASHAR

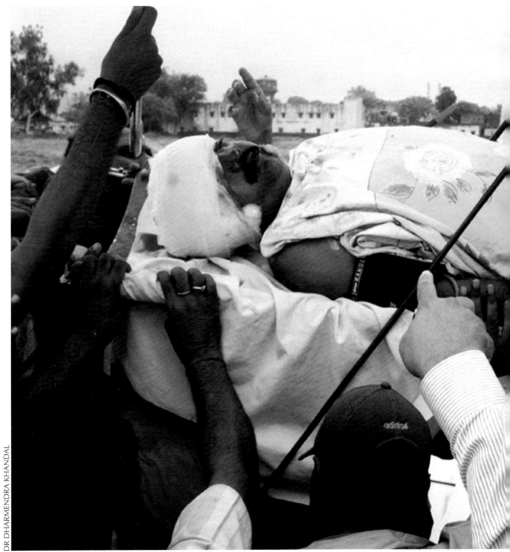

DR DHARMENDRA KHANDAL

for blood transfusion, otherwise I would not survive. I could feel all parts of my body getting stiff through the excruciating pain but I was determined not to lose hope and confidence till I reached the hospital in Sawai Madhopur. That journey of 40 km from Bhuri Pahari to Sawai Madhopur Hospital must have been the longest in my life, or so it seemed at that point in time.

I could hear people talking around me but nothing was clear. In between, I could recognise the voice of ACF Yadav asking me if I was conscious. I could not reply as my mouth was full of blood, the upper part of my nose was completely crushed and blood was flowing from my head into the nostrils and towards my stomach. I murmured to let them know that I was still conscious. Everything after that was a blur and I do not remember anything except asking for sedatives at the hospital and the fact that it was raining when I was airlifted to Jaipur. I also asked about Hukum Chand, Rajveer and Tulsiram, who were with me when the tiger attacked. I was told that they were all right and I drifted into oblivion as the plane took off.

Gravely injured, the author is airlifted from Sawai Madhopur and taken to Jaipur

I was admitted into the Intensive Care Unit of the Sawai Man Singh (SMS) Hospital, Jaipur, for 12 days and was later shifted to the cottage ward for two months. I recollect pointing at my jaw when the doctors were examining me. The right side of my face was totally crushed and there were major injuries on the rest of the face and nose. My jaw was fractured and was operated and tightened by wires for a month. I was breathing and being fed by a pipe through the trachea. I was admitted on 20 August but the major surgery could not be performed before 23 August as they had to wait for 72 hours for the rabies treatment to be complete. I recall the Chief Minister of Rajasthan, Ashok Gehlot, visiting me in the hospital and also other senior forest officers, colleagues, friends and my family, encouraging me and motivating me to hang on as the worst was over.

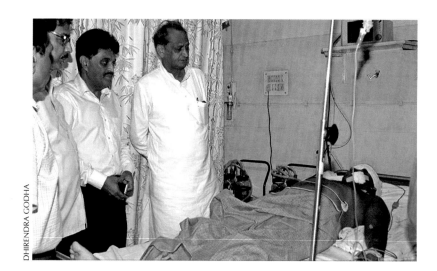

*The Chief Minister of Rajasthan, Ashok Gehlot, at
SMS Hospital, Jaipur*

The single most important factor that kept me going was perhaps the unfinished family responsibilities that I had. My son was working for a multinational firm in South Africa and my daughter was a banker in Gurgaon. I had to get them married and make sure they were well settled before I could die.

When I was being operated on 23 August, I saw the God of Death come to take me away. Whether it was a hallucination or a drug induced dream, I do not know, but it is as vivid today as if it had actually happened. He (God of Death) told me that my time had come to move on to other realms. I countered that I was not ready yet as I had to fulfill a lot of duties before my life could be taken from me. To which he replied that I had battled death like a warrior, so I should not be afraid to die now. He said that death and time waited for no one and I was indeed fortunate to have got some more time to defy death. Hearing his words, sadness overwhelmed me. I thought of my parents, my wife and children with love, then resigned myself to my fate. He told me that I was dying the death of a courageous man and I should be proud of myself. I felt all my worries going away as he started counting backwards from 10. At zero, my life would be snuffed out. I was no longer afraid. It was like I was falling into a deep, dark well and going down into an abyss.

Then, someone caught hold of my hand gently and squeezed it. My eyes flew open and I heard soft voices around me. My wife was holding my hand and telling me that my surgery had gone off well and now I was being taken to the ICU for post-operative care. I could not believe that I was alive and with my family; I even pinched myself just to ensure that I was alive. My son, daughter and some relatives had also arrived. I could not narrate this entire episode, my encounter with the God of Death, as my jaws were closed with wires and I could not speak. I nonetheless wrote to my wife in a register that I needed to tell her something very important as soon as I would be able to speak again.

I was given the best medical treatment possible at the hospital in Jaipur because of the intervention of the seniors in the department and the

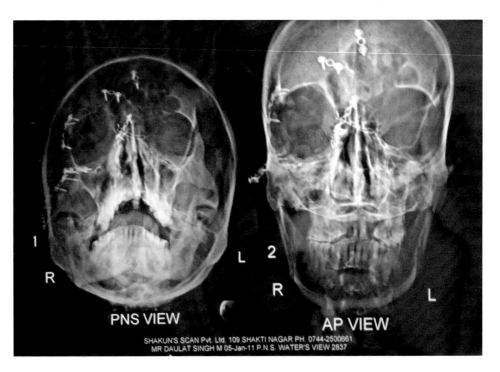

Scans reveal that the right side of the author's face is totally crushed and there are major injuries on the rest of his face and nose, including a fractured jaw

Chief Minister of Rajasthan himself. After being discharged, my treatment continued for the next two to three years. I am grateful to Ravi Singh, Chief Executive Officer, WWF India, for providing financial support for my subsequent eye surgeries at Apollo Hospital, New Delhi. Before that I also went to Mumbai and Ahmedabad for eye treatment. The right side of my skull and face has been reconstructed with three steel plates and 20 screws; till date there is no sensation on this side of the face. My jaws do not work completely and I can chew and eat food only from the left side. My right eye socket has also been reconstructed and an artificial eye placed in it. I can only see with one eye but I strongly believe that it is enough to see the wonders of nature and admire God's work.

I have not been able to figure out this most unforgettable experience with the God of Death, but I am grateful to have been given the opportunity to fulfill my duties. Both my son and daughter are now married and I am also a grandfather to my son's angelic little girl. I have huge respect for life and I want to continue working in the field of conservation and wildlife till my 'time' finally arrives. I hold no grudge against the tiger T-7, who almost mutilated me forever. He attacked me in self-defence, after suffering an ordeal at the hands of the local villagers for hours. Animals do not understand man-made boundaries. T-7 did not know that, when he killed the buffalo for food, he had strayed into human habitation and that he would be harassed for this error by a shouting mob who would repeatedly throw stones at him. They allowed him neither the chance to hide himself among the crops in the field nor permitted him to run back to the safety of the forest. He was more scared than the locals gathered there. The attack on me happened in full view of these people. It must have stunned them as the tiger managed to get away from the spot. He moved away from

A camera trap photograph of T-7, Keoladeo National Park,
13 October 2010

Ranthambhore and travelled more than 200 km towards Karauli and, finally, to Mathura in Uttar Pradesh. All attempts to track and immobilise him were initially unsuccessful. He reached Keoladeo National Park (KNP), Bharatpur, on 10 October 2010, from where he was subsequently translocated to Sariska Tiger Reserve on 23 February 2011.

BHOLU ABRAR KHAN

*T-7 being radio-collared after tranquillising, Keoladeo
National Park, Bharatpur*

Even though I had not yet fully recovered, I joined the team that
tranquillised him and was part of the translocation process along
with RS Shekhawat, Anoop KR, Dr Malik, Dr Shankar, Dr Subhadeep
and the frontline staff of KNP. T-7 is now in Sariska and is known as
the dominant male tiger ST-6.

DINESH YARMA DURRANI

It has been seven years since that encounter, yet some thoughts linger on. There was a large number of forest staff and officials, along with police personnel, present at the time of my accident; the attack happened in full view of most of them. If only they had intervened, or been a little proactive, I may still have retained sight in both my eyes and would be able to utilise my jaw properly. The tiger had first grabbed my hand within his jaws, before he took the right side of my head in his mouth.

As I learnt later, this was when Rajveer, Hukum Chand and Tulsi Ram charged at him with *lathi*s (long sticks). They inflicted blows on his back till he left me and lunged at them. They ran away but saved my life as the tiger also fled after that. If the police, armed with guns, had the foresight of firing in the air or distracting the tiger somehow by moving towards him, in a group, my horror story would have had a different ending. Anyway, *que sera, sera*, whatever will be, will be. I am happy to be alive.

On 15 August 2011, I was presented the Outstanding Service Award by the Chief Minister of Rajasthan in Jaipur. WWF India also honoured me with a citation in New Delhi; a lot of other rewards such as the Sanctuary Asia award and the RBS and Ranthambhore Foundation award were given to me, which certainly boosted my morale.

As is the norm these days, my unfortunate encounter with T-7 got a lot of media attention. Most of it was positive and my courage and dedication to duty were appreciated. However, a section of knowledgeable people were sarcastic about the episode. If people who have no knowledge of the situation merely criticised what had taken place on that eventful day, I would just shrug it off. But if the criticism comes from someone who is well aware of the volatility of the man-animal conflict on the periphery of protected forests, it saddens me deeply.

I was fully aware of the dangers of tracking the tiger on foot, given the situation on 20 August 2010. I have spent all my service years in the wildlife division of the Rajasthan Forest Department, mainly in tiger areas. I am conversant with the behaviour of animals and their volatile nature. We had decided to defer the operation till the crowd dispersed. But the mob there was in a state of frenzy and could not be controlled by the police force and the forest staff. So, I did what was expected of me. I was not imprudent or riding on false bravado to risk my life, just a couple of years before my retirement from service. My ability to tranquillise was also questioned by these critics. Surprisingly, on many other occasions when I have had to sedate and translocate big cats, the very same people have applauded me.

My love for wildlife is genuine; in fact, I cannot even imagine doing any other kind of work, besides being on active field duty in the forests among wild animals. When I re-joined office after the T-7 encounter, I was given a desk job in the Forest Department in Kota, my hometown. I was very unhappy and it was extremely difficult for me to visualise spending the rest of my service years behind a desk, far away from the forest. My family was witness to my misery and they grudgingly agreed to let me ask for an active field posting again.

I was back in the wilderness of Ranthambhore on 16 August 2011, exactly a year after the incident, in surroundings that are inseparable from my soul.

THE STORY OF USTAD

This is the tale of Ustad (T-24), an aggressive male tiger who was born free and lived freely in the Ranthambhore Tiger Reserve. In the prime of his life, this felid occupied a large area of the Reserve, which covered Tourism Zones 1 and 2.

*I*n 2006, Chhindali-Sakdi tigress (T-22) gave birth to her last litter of three male cubs. Their father was Jhumru (T-20), who maintained a large territory in the Khandar, Gilaisagar, Lahpur, Guda, Pandudah and Kisnidah areas of the Ranthambhore Tiger Reserve. One summer morning in 2008, I witnessed the tigress with her three children at the Langdi Mata Ka Chatta waterhole. My arrival disturbed the mother and they moved into the thickets nearby. Determined to get a good look and take pictures of the family, we waited patiently in my Gypsy. I knew that it would not be long before the cubs would leave their mother to carve out territories of their own and this could well be the last time I saw them together. We waited patiently for almost an hour before we saw one cub venturing out. He looked in our direction, growled, then moved into the waterhole. Emboldened by their sibling, soon the other two cubs also came out and proceeded to the waterhole. The mother followed. The cubs frolicked around in the water, playfully jumping at each other and their indulgent mother. I clicked away happily. I observed that one of them was more aggressive than the others. He would periodically look towards us, growl and then go back to playing with the family. This sub-adult male was later named Ustad (T-24).

Sub-adult tigers frolicking in the water, playfully jumping at each other, with their indulgent mother

DAULAT SINGH SHAKTAWAT

One of the tigers would periodically growl and then go back to playing with the family. This sub-adult male was later named Ustad

DAULAT SINGH SHAKTAWAT

Early in 2009, Ustad moved out of the Reserve and traversed to Chidi Kho and Jamoda in the adjoining Sawai Mansingh Sanctuary. On 23 April 2009, I was informed by the Sanctuary staff that they had seen Ustad with his left forelimb badly swollen, probably due to some injury. In the case of an injury to wild animals, we generally allow nature to take its course and find that they are soon healed. They are, after all, wild animals living in their natural surroundings and the law of the jungle must prevail. But, sometimes, if an injury or disability is observed in a predator, we have to intervene because it may hinder its ability to hunt for food. It is said that a tiger often attempts to bring down a prey many times before he can actually get his meal. For this, he has to be absolutely fit. Disturbed by the news of Ustad's injury, I rushed to the Sawai Mansingh Sanctuary to see the tiger I had been following since his birth.

I spotted him near a waterhole at Chidi Kho. I focused my camera at his forelimb and zoomed in. He had a big wound on the pad of his front left paw. We reported this to the Deputy Director of the Ranthambhore Tiger Reserve, RS Shekhawat. After debating for a while, we decided to tranquillise him to take a look at the wound and subsequently treat it. The local veterinarian, Dr Rajeev Garg and his team were with us when I shot the tranquillising dart at Ustad. As the dart hit the rump, the tiger got up, took a short leap and crossed the adjacent four feet high, dry stone wall and disappeared into the bushes. We waited for 15 minutes and then carefully moved in the direction of the tiger. Forest guard Rajveer and I found him lying on the ground 50 to 60 metres away from us. He was huge and looked majestic and fierce, even in this tranquillised state. Just

Ustad at a waterhole
in the Sawai Mansingh
Sanctuary after separating
from his family

DAULAT SINGH SHAKTAWAT

to be sure, we threw a few pebbles at him and he promptly raised his head. We retreated quickly and shot him another small dose to sedate him completely. Another wait of 15 minutes and he was sleeping soundly. The earlier dose had been given on the assumption of a body weight of about 200 kg, the norm for a healthy three-year-old male tiger. But Ustad was bigger, 224 kg, as we found out later when we weighed him.

The author follows Ustad in order to sedate him
so that his injury could be treated

*Checking to see whether Ustad is unconscious. He is then
covered by a wet gunny cloth to keep him cool*

Dr Garg quickly started his work. He made an incision on the paw and
cleaned out the pus. Antibiotics and other medicines were injected and
he was radio-collared. Ustad was then transferred to a cage for 48 hours
of observation. This cage was placed near the Chidi Kho waterhole.

After two days, the tiger was sedated again and further medication was administered. Just when Udayram, Range Officer of Phalodi, started rubbing an ice pack on the wounded paw, Ustad lifted his head and looked around. Everyone panicked and ran away. The tiger was left lying on the stretcher with bandages on his forelimb. Ustad got up, took a few unsteady strides and sat down again. The effect of the sedation had not completely worn off but it was too dangerous to go near him or to tranquillise him further. So we kept our distance and observed him through the night. Around midnight, we saw him go to the waterhole.

We were worried that if his bandaged limb got submerged in water it would aggravate the infection. But, to our amazement, Ustad went into the waterhole, put his hind legs in first, then the entire body, only the bandaged left forelimb was kept out of water!

We continued with our vigil to make sure that he had recovered fully. The next morning, Ustad moved into the forest and we saw him as evening was falling, walking leisurely on a forest track. His gait seemed so normal that it confused us. Was it Ustad or some other tiger? Closer observation confirmed that it was Ustad, indeed. Two days later, he killed an adult blue bull in the interior *nallah* of Chidi Kho. Ustad had returned to stalk and hunt his prey again. After one year, by early 2010, he moved to the peripheral areas of Jhoomar Baori of the Ranthambhore Tiger Reserve.

It was around this time that the errant behaviour of Ustad started.

On 3 July 2010, I received an urgent message from Mohanlal Garg, a forester from Rajbag. He had been carrying out routine patrolling on

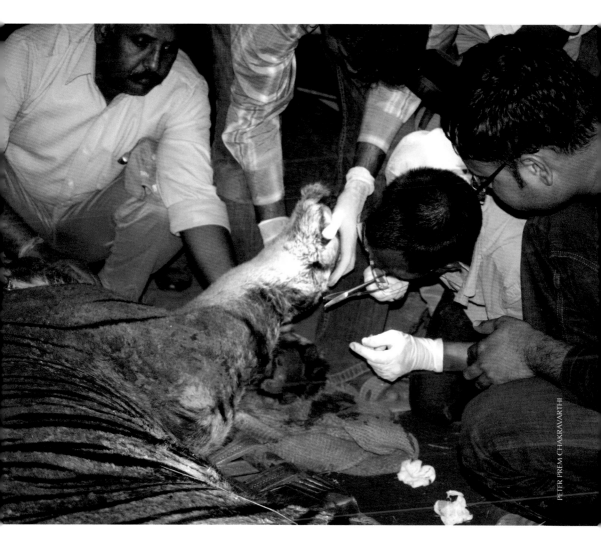

PETER PREM CHAKRAVARTHI

*The author provides a helping hand while Ustad's paw is
treated by Dr Rajeev Garg and his team*

foot with his team in the Jhoomar Baori area, when they came across a recently-cut dhonk tree and a blood-stained axe lying next to it. Mohanlal was aware that a person (Ghamandilal) from Sawai Madhopur, who had gone to collect fuel wood, was missing. Mohanlal investigated further and found a pair of yellow, blood-stained slippers. He feared the worst and sent me an urgent wireless message.

As soon as I reached the Jhoomar Baori area, I divided my team of six into two groups and we started combing the place. Soon I came across the spot with the partially cut dhonk tree where the tiger had probably attacked the man. I sent a wireless message to RS Shekhawat and continued with the combing operations. We found drag marks leading to blood-stained clothes near a stone fencing on top of a hillock. Drag marks were visible on the other side of the dry stone fencing, going into the dense bushes. This area

DAULAT SINGH SHAKTAWAT

Wild animals rarely attack humans unprovoked; it is aberrant behaviour

was close to the boundary of the Reserve, along the Ranthambhore road. The Deputy Director and ACF Yadav also joined us there. We had a quick discussion and decided to go ahead with our search for the body of the unfortunate victim. Ustad had been radio-collared earlier so we thought it would be a good idea to check his whereabouts as this area was his territory. Evening was setting in when we got signals from the radio collar, leading us to the bush with drag marks. We could not wait any longer as it would be dangerous as well as difficult to search in the darkness for the predator and the victim. Meanwhile, the police were trying to keep the local crowds away from us. With heavy hearts, Deputy Director Shekhawat, ACF Yadav and I, along with a handful of frontline staff, started walking slowly within the bushy undergrowth. We had *lathi*s in our hands and were making a lot of noise as we crept ahead. We

DAULAT SINGH SHAKTAWAT

crossed the bushes and moved on to an open area. There, under a raunj tree, we saw something that shook us up: a naked, blood-covered human body. The predator was nowhere in sight so we managed to wrap up the body and carry it back to the police and the angry crowd. The body was identified as Ghamandilal and it was handed over to the police for the necessary formalities.

In spite of having spent my entire working life in active field postings in the wildlife areas of Rajasthan, I still reel back in shock and sadness whenever a mishap like this occurs. I have never seen wild animals attacking humans unprovoked; it is aberrant behaviour. Sadness enveloped me because, whatever be the reason, it was a tragic loss of human life.

After this incident, thorough monitoring and tracking of Ustad was started. Since he was radio-collared, it was not difficult to keep an update of his whereabouts every day. It was the end of July and still too hot for tigers to move up to the hilltops during the daytime but I saw Ustad almost always on the top, in the Jhoomar Baori area, during the early mornings and late evenings. Even on hot sunny days, he could be seen on this hilltop. Perhaps he

As Ustad was radio-collared, it was not difficult to keep an update of his whereabouts

DAULAT SINGH SHAKTAWAT

was avoiding contact with the dominant T-12 male tiger who had his territory in the valley areas.

Seventeen days after the Ghamandilal mishap, T-12 was translocated to the Sariska Tiger Reserve. This was an opportunity for Ustad to extend his territory, but he took his time to begin roaming in the Singhdwar, Raipur and Sultanpur areas. Gradually, he started moving around there and also in Tourism Zones 1 and 2.

On the first day of joining duty after I was attacked by T-7, I went straight to visit the Ranthambhore Tiger Reserve forest. On the way to Raipur from Singhdwar, I found Ustad sitting at the tri-junction, next to a sambar kill. He looked healthy and like a fully grown adult. I was told that he had also acquired a new partner recently, T-39 (Noor). This couple became so dominant in the area that they pushed out another tigress, T-13, mother of T-39, and her two cubs, to the Sawai Mansingh Sanctuary. Ustad and Noor began to reign supreme over the Sultanpur and Guda areas of Tourism Zones 1 and 2. We were even expecting to see cubs soon from their prolonged courtship.

Ustad at a waterhole in Tourism Zone No. 2 at the Ranthambhore Tiger Reserve

Mother bear with cubs in a fight with Ustad

ADITYA SINGH

DAULAT SINGH SHAKTAWAT

*Ustad moving around the Pandu Deh and
Krishna Deh areas marking territory*

DAULAT SINGH SHAKTAWAT

On 9 March 2012, we were informed by the personnel at Rajbag Naka that a young man, Ashfaq, had gone to the neighbouring forests, but had not returned. We searched and found a mutilated human body on a rocky surface surrounded by thorny thickets. Locals accompanying us confirmed that it was Ashfaq. It could have been the work of any wild carnivore, but, a short distance away, on the mud track, we found the pugmarks of a big male tiger. Ustad was the only dominant male occupying that area.

It was later that year, on 21 May 2012, that Noor was spotted with a single male cub. Since he was the only cub born to this tigress, he got his mother's full attention and was growing well. He was named Sultan. I saw Sultan many times, along with his mother and father, Ustad, playing and jumping around. By the end of 2012, Ustad, Noor and Sultan had occupied the entire Tourism Zones 1 and 2 as well as a part of Zone 6. The trio could often be seen together by the

Ustad had become quite familiar with humans from his early days of territory establishment

DAULAT SINGH SHAKTAWAT

forest staff. On 25 October 2012, we got news that one of our assistant foresters, Ghishu Singh, had been attacked by a tiger near the Naya Kalapani anicut when he was supervising two groups of labourers near the anicut and Sohan Kachch. While walking from one group to the other, Ghishu was suddenly attacked by a tiger who took him away. The labourers and staff members heard a muffled cry and feared the worst. On reaching there, Deputy Field Director YK Sahu and the staff members found Ustad sitting on a hill slope opposite a *nallah*, at a distance of 50 to 60 metres from the jeep road. Close to him lay the dead body of Ghishu Singh. To scare Ustad away, vehicles were moved closer to him and horns were blared but he did not budge. After a while, he got up and moved to the dead body. Gypsy horns were blown incessantly while the staff shouted and thumped the ground with *lathis* to distract the tiger. Finally, he moved languorously towards the forest on the hillside. Vehicles were quickly moved next to the body to retrieve it. This incident really shook up the entire frontline staff of the Reserve; they were now scared to venture anywhere in Ustad's territory. I also

Members of the field staff patrolling with the Field Director (second from right) and Ghishu Singh (fourth from left)

DAULAT SINGH SHAKTAWAT

noticed a change in Ustad's behaviour. Three days after the incident, I was on night patrol when I saw him on the main road, between the Singhdwar and Mishr Darra gate. He stopped, looked at our vehicle and kept gazing at us for a long time, without any fear. I observed Ustad on many other occasions after that and noticed that same boldness. It seemed that the presence of humans did not bother him. As a matter of fact, he had become quite familiar with humans from his early days of territory establishment. All along Tourism Zones 1 and 2, a large number of pilgrims used to walk from the Sherpur tri-junction of Ranthambhore to the Ganesh Temple and the Parikrama Road circling the Ranthambhore Fort. Therefore, already familiar with human presence, Ustad, now, after these three incidents, had became completely devoid of the fear of humans.

Generally, tigers are solitary animals but seeing this family of three (Ustad, Noor and Sultan) together made me believe that tigers have a social life. I was fortunate to capture these family moments with my camera. While Noor taught Sultan how to hunt in the wild, Ustad could often be seen 'scolding' his son for his naughtiness. When Sultan was a sub-adult, I

Ustad at a waterhole

once found him being aggressive towards his father after sharing a sambar kill. At first Ustad tolerated him but when Sultan tried to approach him to show further dominance, Ustad simply roared like a thunderstorm. Ustad, being the father, did not attack him physically but his roaring was good enough to literally make Sultan pee. Thereafter, Sultan was so scared that he was totally in awe of his father. The same day, he left his natal area and moved towards the peripheral areas of the Ranthambhore Tiger Reserve and, after staying there for a few days, finally moved on to the Keladevi Wildlife Sanctuary.

The last incident that seems to have sealed Ustad's fate occurred on 8 May 2015. It was past 6 pm when I received a call from the booking barrier of Ranthambhore that forest guard Rampal Mali, deputed at that checkpost, had been attacked by a tiger near Atal Sagar, next to the Ranthambhore road. I rushed to the spot and saw Rampal Mali being taken to the hospital by other staff members. As advised by the Deputy Conservator of Forests (DCF) of the Ranthambhore Tiger Reserve, Sudarshan Sharma, I proceeded to the accident spot with Dr Dharmendra Khandal of Tiger Watch and Aditya Singh, along with the barrier post staff members. We

DAULAT SINGH SHAKTAWAT

Ustad making his presence felt across the Reserve

DAULAT SINGH SHAKTAWAT

*Father and son enjoying each other's company
as they play together. When Ustad was challenged by his son Sultan,
he attacked him in jest*

DAULAT SINGH SHAKTAWAT

Sultan, it seems, rubbed his nose on the ground, only then did Ustad allow him to leave. Ustad could often be seen 'scolding' his son for his naughtiness

DAULAT SINGH SHAKTAWAT

Sultan moved to the periphery after the episode with his father

found fresh blood stains on an animal track going towards the forest from the main road and started searching the adjoining areas in the hope of finding evidence of tiger movement. Meanwhile, the flying squad of Ranthambhore, which had also arrived at the accident spot, messaged us about the presence of a tiger there. We took about five to seven minutes to reach and found a male tiger coming out on the same blood-stained track we had seen earlier. He kept sniffing at the blood on the ground. We managed to divert the tourist and Ganesh Temple vehicles to the Ranthambhore road, just as the tiger disappeared behind the wall, next to Atal Sagar near the main road. Bikers were told to park their vehicles and wait inside the rooms at the Mishr Darra gate. Soon, the tiger came out again on the main road, scent-marked it and started moving towards the gate.

We were behind the tiger, following him from a safe distance. Suddenly, our driver braked as we crossed Mishr Darra. Dr Khandal, who was sitting next to me, fell off! We quickly helped him to get back onto the Gypsy and reversed the vehicle. The tiger heard the sound of Dr Khandal falling and retraced his steps to come back towards us. Dr Khandal's spectacles were lying on the road. The tiger walked up to them, sniffed and then moved towards Tourism Zone 1. We later tracked his movement up to Sultanpur. Though it was evening, we had seen the tiger clearly; we had even taken photographs to confirm his identity. It was Ustad, without a doubt.

Ustad's behaviour may not be like that of a man-eater but it was definitely not that of a normal tiger as well. Usually, tigers avoid encounters with humans. Several times, while tracking on foot, I have come across tigers, but in nine cases out of ten, the tiger has moved away. Ustad, however, was

Ustad had probably realised the vulnerability of humans as easy prey whenever he encountered them at close proximity

DAULAT SINGH SHAKTAWAT

totally unafraid of humans. It seemed that he had probably realised the vulnerability of humans as easy prey whenever he encountered them at close proximity. It was a scary situation, not only for the frontline staff of the Reserve but also for tourists and pilgrims. We could not allow any other disaster to happen. So, the difficult decision to tranquillise Ustad and to shift him away was taken. This was done on 16 May 2015.

It is indeed sad to see a healthy tiger, used to roaming freely and reigning supreme over a large territory in the wild, now confined inside a cage in a zoological park. Yet, this sometimes becomes a necessity when there is really no other option. Ustad's narrative, with its several turns and twists, is testimony to this.

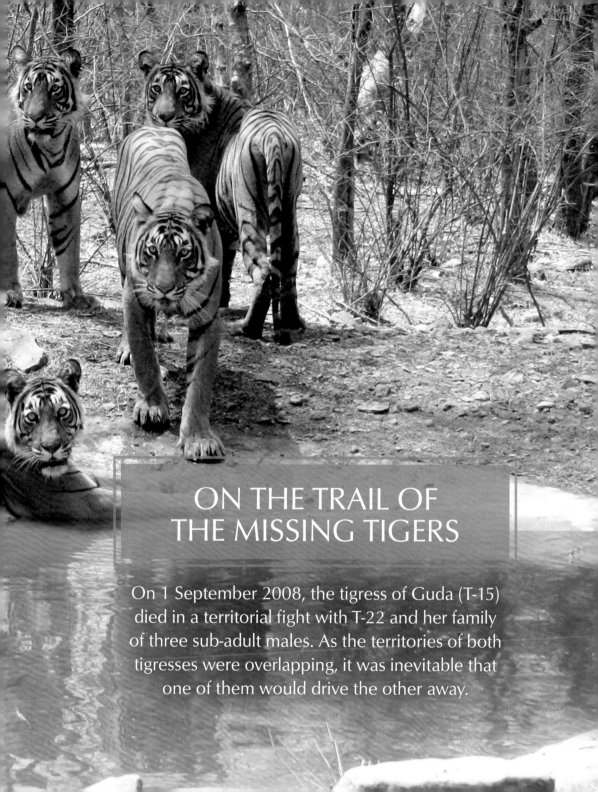

ON THE TRAIL OF
THE MISSING TIGERS

On 1 September 2008, the tigress of Guda (T-15)
died in a territorial fight with T-22 and her family
of three sub-adult males. As the territories of both
tigresses were overlapping, it was inevitable that
one of them would drive the other away.

𝓤nfortunately, T-15 had two small cubs, a male and a female, about seven to eight months old. The survival of such young cubs in the wild, without their mother, seemed almost impossible. It was now up to us, the forest staff of Ranthambhore, to ensure their well-being. I made my temporary headquarters at Guda Chowki with the intent of tracking and monitoring the cubs from the day their mother had died. We formed three groups to keep a close check on them and, initially, we found their pugmarks in and around the area their mother had died. Both

DAULAT SINGH SHAKTAWAT

T-15 tigress with her cubs,
T-36 and T-37

T-36 and T-37 after the death of their mother, T-15,
in the Guda region

DAULAT SINGH SHAKTAWAT

DAULAT SINGH SHAKTAWAT

*T-15 with T-36 cub:
The survival of young
cubs in the wild,
without their mother,
seems impossible*

DAULAT SINGH SHAKTAWAT

cubs did not come out during the day so there were very few instances of direct sighting. We tried to provide food for them by placing goat meat in the area. A camera trap was installed to monitor their whereabouts.

We would often find evidence that the meat had been taken away by hyenas. After some time, we started putting small live baits for the cubs to kill. Each time the bait was taken, we would check for the siblings'

The flehmen response: T-15 tigress with her cubs, T-36 and T-37

DAULAT SINGH SHAKTAWAT

Cubs with their mother, T-15

pugmarks and jump in celebration when we found evidence of the cubs killing and dragging the bait. This carried on for nearly a month when, suddenly, the cubs disappeared.

Undoubtedly, territorial pressure from other adult tigers in the Guda area, particularly the tigress of Jogi Mahal (T-18), made the cubs move away. Sustained foot patrolling for the next five days yielded no results and we

T-36 and T-37 exploring the Guda region

were unsuccessful in locating them. I discussed the movement pattern of these cubs and their mother with the Guda staff. I was informed that their mother had taken them to Mansarovar a couple of times and from there towards Indala through Mirchighati. The personnel at Indala Chowki were told to look out for the cubs, but there was no movement there.

On the sixth day, I set out with my staff and followed the same track through Mirchighati. Near a waterhole, right at the top, we found hundreds of pugmarks made by the cubs. We were overjoyed and quickly arranged a live bait for them. The bait was taken the following day! It was such a relief to know that the cubs were alive and doing well. However, the cubs

T-18, female tigress of
Jogi Mahal, occupies
the Guda area

moved again, this time to the Langdi Mata Temple and Chindali, adjacent to Guda. Sometimes the forest staff would see them feeding on the kill left by the T-22 family.

Soon the cubs had to move again because of the dominant T-18 tigress. Both the cubs were photographed on 5 December 2008 at a chital kill in the Kishni Dah area. They remained around that vicinity for another four days, then separated. During the morning tracking on 9 December, pugmarks of the female cub were seen from Mordungri to Mansarovar, going towards the Sawai Mansingh Sanctuary. The male cub, however, was found roaming in Nalghati and Guda. He was then spotted near the Jogi Mahal, Lakkarda, Anatpura and Jhoomar Bawari areas where he stayed for a few days. These regions in the National Park were already occupied by dominant male tigers. Therefore, the sub-adult male finally left the forest on 6 February 2009 and moved towards the agricultural fields near Sawai Madhopur Railway Colony where he started killing pigs and small domestic cattle.

It was an extremely difficult time for my range staff and me. The tiger had moved into the vicinity of human habitation where someone or the other would often spot him, raise a hue and cry and throw

SR YADAV

124

The cubs had to move again because of the dominant T-18 tigress

S.R.YADAV

us into a frenzy. A disaster could be waiting to happen. We spent many sleepless nights in agricultural fields and guava orchards, trying to monitor the tiger and push him towards the forest, but with no luck. We tried hard to find him so that we could tranquillise him but it was impossible as the crops in the fields were standing tall, providing him full cover. The guava orchards surrounding the fields were also dense, thus inhibiting visibility still further. Meanwhile, the local people were panicking; they were scared to go to their fields and had started agitating against the Forest Department.

It was early in the morning on 3 March 2009 when I received a message from the Ramsinghpura forest guard that the tiger had entered a farm with five to six feet high mustard crops. The farm had a *pucca* (solid, permanent) masonry wall, six feet high, around it and was just behind the Abrar Palace hotel on Ranthambhore road. By the time I reached there, the news of the tiger hiding inside the farm had spread like wildfire and locals and tourists were flocking to the area. Some even climbed the boundary wall to get a glimpse of the tiger. The situation was extremely precarious with noisy crowds of people on the one hand and an agitated, cornered tiger on the other. Suddenly, the tiger mock-charged at the people standing on the wall! Fortunately, they fell on the other side of the boundary, quite shaken but unhurt.

Staff members and vehicles were deputed to the outside of the wall to control the mob and monitor the tiger's movement. I, too, waited to pick up some movement from the tiger. The whole day had passed without us getting a glimpse of the tiger and soon it would be dark. We had to act fast. I could not wait any longer and asked my driver to cover the Gypsy with its hood and move on. We took the vehicle within the mustard field where the tiger was hiding.

Tall crops enveloped our vehicle and we moved ahead with difficulty. It was impossible to see beyond two to three metres. Dusk had also fallen. How could we locate the tiger? With a heavy heart, we got out of the mustard field to find that most of the people had moved away as dusk had now given way to darkness. Our staff was still surrounding the area and keeping watch with searchlights. We knew that we had to wait patiently for the tiger to make the first move.

At around 10 pm, the tiger jumped over the wall, crossed the Abrar Palace hotel and disappeared into the outer fencing of the Oberoi Vanyavilas.

T-36 resting inside the outer fencing of the Oberoi Vanyavilas hotel

DAULAT SINGH SHAKTAWAT

This created further excitement among the guests and staff of the hotel, who came out to watch the tiger. We were hoping that the tiger would move across the right side of the fenced area into the jungle, but he did no such thing. Troubled by the crowds and his day-long ordeal, he was now agitated and aggressive. He paced up and down inside the fencing.

We requested everyone to stay indoors and started beating drums from the opposite end so that he would move to the forested areas on the right. All attempts to move him eventually failed. Then, at 4 am, he suddenly jumped over the fence and was gone in a flash. At daybreak, we tracked his pugmarks and discovered that he had gone back into the guava orchards after crossing the railway line. This was proving to be one of the more difficult operations I had handled.

A tranquillising team from the Wildlife Institute of India (WII), Dehradun, was summoned to assist us. We searched for the tiger for four days and three nights, but could not spot him. His pugmarks, though, assured us that he was still around. The WII team went back disappointed and we continued with our efforts.

It was now March 2009 and crops had to be harvested from the fields, but our tiger was still at large in the area adjoining the Railway Colony. On 21 March, at 6 am, I got a wireless message that a woman had been attacked by a sub-adult tiger in the fields near the Railway Colony. The tiger had then turned and disappeared back into the fields. Deputy Director RS Shekhawat, ACF Sudarshan Sharma and I formed three teams and spread out in different directions to track the attacker. We discovered fresh pugmarks but after a point they stopped; the ACF's team also reached where we were and saw the pugmarks disappearing. We decided to comb the area again and carefully look into each and every bush and shrub as the tiger could not have simply vanished.

Suddenly, Nirbhay Singh, a forest guard, shouted that he had seen the tiger crouching in a bush. Before we could reach the spot, the tiger pounced at Nirbhay. We ran in different directions but stopped in our tracks when we heard a scream. Forester Mohanlal was the closest to the tiger and, as he turned, the tiger lashed out at him with his claws. When we saw the charging tiger, we started shouting and throwing stones to scare him away. Horrified, we saw Mohanlal falling down. Shouting loudly, we rushed towards the tiger; the sudden movement of people and the loud noise made by us succeeded in scaring him away. He took one jump and disappeared.

Mohanlal was bleeding because of the claw marks on his back. He was in a state of shock and his blood pressure was falling. I tried to reassure him that he was safe and would be fine after proper medical care. Having made arrangements for him to be sent to the local hospital immediately, we turned our attention back to the tiger who had now become more aggressive after being attacked with stones. The Railway Colony wall was broken in one place where we found pugmarks. The colony compound was covered with thick *Prosopis juliflora* bushes, so searching for him was not going to be easy. We drove around in my Gypsy, flattening some bushes, peeping in at others. We were moving at a slow speed when we heard the snarl of the tiger. Then I spotted his ears behind a bush, close to a *nallah*. The rest of him was covered by the bush. We switched off the engine of the vehicle and waited for him to emerge so that I could get a shot at him with my tranquillising gun. But this tiger, it seemed, had developed the knack of making things difficult for us. We kept waiting. It was almost 1 pm and the tiger had not moved. A sizeable crowd had collected and was perched on rooftops, walls and a water tank. The police were doing their best to keep them in check. Thankfully, the rising heat of the afternoon made the crowd gradually move away.

Some people who were still sitting on the top of the tank shouted that the tiger was moving towards the Railway Colony houses. Following him in the Gypsy was impossible. So, I, along with two team members, ran into the colony from a side street and climbed onto the terrace of a house.

DR DHARMENDRA KHANDAL

T-36 being loaded in a truck after tranquillisation
Below: A huge crowd gathers at the Railway Colony during the tranquillisation of T-36

I could now get a clear view. The tiger was sitting behind a bush, stalking a cow grazing nearby. I took aim and shot the dart at its rump. It struck him and he roared and ran back to where he had been hiding earlier. It was 1:25 pm. We waited for 15 minutes and then drove towards him. I threw small pebbles at the tiger when I saw him lying under a bush; he did not budge. The medicine had worked and he was totally immobilised. We quickly moved in with the veterinarian, Dr Rajeev Garg, lifted the tiger on a stretcher and transferred him to a cage. Before moving the cage to our office, we covered it with a wet cloth to keep the tiger's temperature down. We radio-collared him in our office compound and gave him the antidote injection for revival.

After an hour, we started towards the Sawai Mansingh Sanctuary to release him. Meanwhile, we kept splashing water on the cloth covering the cage. By the time we reached the Aantri forest area of the Sanctuary, it was 4:30 pm and the tiger, now fully conscious, was roaring inside.

DAULAT SINGH SHAKTAWAT

DAULAT SINGH SHAKTAWAT

Facing page: T-36 being radio-collared
Above: Being released in the Sawai Mansingh Sanctuary

T-37 in the Qualji area

I positioned myself at a vantage point from where I could get a clear view and signalled to my staff to slowly open the gate of the cage. The tiger took out his head, looked around, gave a deafening roar, jumped and sped away into the jungle. I heaved a sigh of relief; my errant ward had finally gone home.

T-36 in his new surroundings in the Qualji area

Later, the tiger moved towards the southern part of the Ranthambhore Critical Tiger Habitat and developed Qualji as his territory. His sister also joined him there. Both tigers were given identification numbers, the male was T-36 and his sister, T-37.

THE MYSTIFYING LEOPARD

It was 14 October 2009. I left my home in Sawai Madhopur at 5:30 am as always and went patrolling and inspecting the forest areas near Kala-Pila-Pani and Raipur. It was peaceful; the wild denizens seemed to be enjoying the early autumn sun and were coming out into the open to bask near the water bodies.

$\mathcal{A}$ feeling of tranquillity and well-being enveloped me as I moved away from these surroundings that I loved and knew so well. I drove out of the Mishr Darra gate at around 10:30 am and settled down at the barrier forest *chowki* (post) for some mundane work.

The leopard moving around the area of the Mishr Darra gate

DAULAT SINGH SHAKTAWAT

But what transpired thereafter was far from mundane. It was, in fact, so strange that it remains etched in my memory as if it had happened just yesterday.

I was going to begin examining the files and registers, when an excited staff member burst into my room. A leopard had attacked two bikers who were going to the Ganesh Temple on the *pucca* road near the Mishr Darra gate at 8 am. The bikers had been taken to the Sawai Madhopur Hospital for treatment. That was odd. I had gone down the same route and everything seemed normal, with pilgrims proceeding towards the temple in their vehicles.

I immediately went back to the Mishr Darra gate with some members of my staff and closely inspected the forest areas alongside. We could not spot any leopard or find traces of movement. Instructing my staff to stay stationed there and continue patrolling, I went to the hospital to get a first-hand account from the bikers of what had happened that morning.

Fortunately, they were not grievously injured and were able to narrate the incident lucidly and in great detail. They told me that both of them were on one bike and were driving at a speed of 30 kmph on the *pucca* road to the Ganesh Temple. They had just crossed the Mishr Darra gate when, suddenly, a leopard emerged from the forest, which was on the right side of the road and pounced on them. Caught totally unaware by the attack, the two fell on the road. In a split second, the leopard was on them, snarling and attacking.

Their screams and shouts did not deter the leopard as they tried to fight back. It must have taken just a few minutes before other pilgrims collected there and started throwing stones at the leopard. This probably distracted the animal who left them and moved away. But what was truly weird was that even the shouting, stone-throwing, angry mob did not really seem to scare the leopard as he did not leap away. He took one look at the mob and his two victims, turned and walked away leisurely towards the small forested ridge he had come from. He was surely possessed by some evil spirit, they concluded.

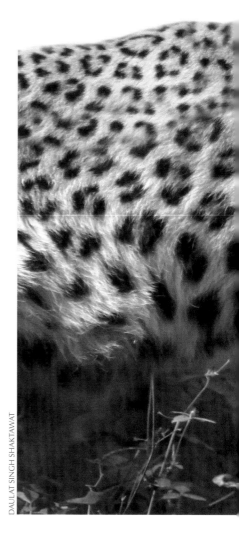

DAULAT SINGH SHAKTAWAT

The leopard was seen moving near the Mishr Darra gate prior to the incident

On the way back from the hospital to my office, I pondered over what the youths had told me. The behaviour of the leopard was inexplicable. In all my years of service, I had never come across a leopard who waited, stalked and attacked humans and that, too, in broad daylight on a road with a regular flow of traffic.

Leopards are often periphery dwellers, no doubt, and are more familiar (as compared to the tiger) with human presence. But they do not come into direct conflict or contact with humans. They are shy, secretive and more elusive. Leopards sometimes prey on dogs and other small livestock in villages on the edge of forests but they almost always hunt in the dark. They move so swiftly and cleverly that before the prey can even let out a yelp or a bleat, the predator has gone off into the forest with his prize. Humans mostly discover the disappearance of their stock or poultry next morning and conclude that a leopard is 'at work' from the presence of pugmarks.

It seemed almost unbelievable that such a smooth operator would appear in daylight and attack humans fearlessly. It could be that the bikers were lying; I speculated that they may have deviated from the tar road onto the jungle track in the hope of sighting something big and chanced upon the leopard, who, in self-defence, charged on them. This conjecture seemed more plausible to me than a leopard willfully attacking humans. I had nearly convinced myself of this theory when I entered my office but news of another leopard attack on a biker on the Mishr Darra road jolted me into action. I messaged the forest *chowki* to block the entry of pedestrians to the Ganesh Temple and to stop all traffic from coming into that area. Once again, I proceeded to the site of the attack. I was on

Leopards are periphery dwellers and are more familiar (as compared to the tiger) with human presence

my way when I received another message. This time, two staff members, who were stopping traffic and guarding the area, were attacked by the leopard. One of them was badly mauled. It was shocking! Within a space of a few hours, the leopard had attacked three times in full daylight on the main road and had only moved away after stones were thrown at him. I reached the barrier *chowki*, told forester Hukum Chand and another staff member to accompany me. We armed ourselves with *lathi*s before moving to the Mishr Darra gate.

The three of us kept a sharp lookout for the leopard in the forest that was bordering the road on both sides and had nearly reached the Mishr Darra gate when Hukum Chand shouted that he had spotted the cat. The leopard was sitting near a Hanuman idol on the platform next to the gate. Seated close to a rock, he was watching our movements. I took out my camera to photograph him and instructed my staff to exercise caution and to be ready with *lathi*s. We were barely 10 to 15 metres away from the animal. I started clicking photographs when I suddenly saw the leopard charging

Shy, secretive and more elusive than tigers, leopards almost always hunt in the dark

DAULAT SINGH SHAKTAWAT

towards us. We swung our *lathis* around, beating them on the Gypsy to make a thumping noise. Deftly avoiding the sticks, the leopard crossed us and moved to the other side of the road. It was clear from the way he had attacked us that his action was not defensive, his intention was to injure us. I had never seen anything like this during my service of over thirty years.

I immediately called up the headquarters at Sawai Madhopur and asked them to send the tranquillising kit urgently. Meanwhile, we came out of the Mishr Darra gate to locate the leopard's movements. He was not in sight. We waited and, within half-an-hour, he came out on the main

DAULAT SINGH SHAKTAWAT

Taking refuge in the adjoining hillside forest

road and strolled towards the gate, as if to challenge us. Deputy Director RS Shekhawat and ACF Sudarshan Sharma soon arrived with the equipment. The leopard had now moved to the left side of the gate, near a Shiva *linga*, above a twelve feet deep water body. He was standing next to the *linga* and snarling at us. We had to decide quickly whether to shoot the dart at him right then or to wait for him to move away as there was the risk of him falling into the pond. We waited for some time but he did not budge. The afternoon safari to the Park was about to start and we were holding up the traffic. So we decided to go ahead with tranquillising him.

With the Shiva linga

The tranquillising dart takes its effect and the leopard slumps down, unconscious

DAULAT SINGH SHAKTAWAT

I took aim and shot the dart at the animal's rump. The dart hit the target and the leopard rose up in fury. He grabbed the *linga* in his mouth and bit down on it hard. He was now bleeding from the mouth. We could do nothing but watch and wait for the medicine to kick in. Thankfully, it took its effect in a few minutes and the leopard slumped down, unconscious. We quickly shifted him onto a stretcher and then into a vehicle and took him to the barrier *chowki*.

The veterinarian, Dr Rajiv Garg, was waiting for our entourage at the *chowki*. It was discovered that the leopard had a deep wound on his back. Antibiotics were sprayed on the wound and some were injected. After the physical examination was done and the medication completed, the leopard was transferred to a cage and the antidote to bring him to consciousness was administered. He soon regained consciousness and started pacing up and down the cage; it seemed as if he was very hungry. A live bait was arranged and put inside the cage. Generally, the bait is devoured immediately in such cases but this leopard continued sitting on one side of the cage while the bait stood in the opposite corner. This was indeed strange behaviour, once again. The leopard then advanced slowly and caught one leg of the bait in his mouth. We all moved away quietly to allow him to have his meal in peace.

We, too, sat down to have a cup of tea. But soon we realised that there was no sound coming from the cage. This definitely warranted a look. The leopard was sitting in one corner while the bait, still alive, except for a chewed-up leg, was at the other end. We covered the cage with a carpet to give them privacy and left them to their fate. I went back to my headquarters with instructions to the staff to maintain a vigil but keep away from the cage. At 11 pm, I went back to re-check on the leopard. I was told that he was lying down on one side of the cage and the bait was still alive. I looked and found the leopard lying still; there was no movement. Picking up a stick, I poked him with it but there was no movement. I looked closely. I could not detect any heaving up and down of the chest, there was no breathing. The leopard was dead!

Next morning, a post-mortem was conducted by a medical board. I requested them to send a sample of the leopard's brain to the Indian Veterinary Research Institute (IVRI) in Bareilly. I had a suspicion. The behaviour of the leopard had been totally out of character; in fact, it had been abnormal. He might have been rabid. I had earlier experienced abnormal behaviour of hyenas in Sariska and, when the brain sample of

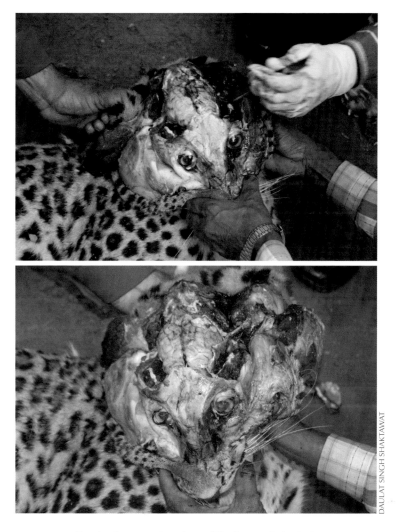

DAULAT SINGH SHAKTAWAT

*Conducting a postmortem of the leopard's brain to
determine the cause of his unusual behaviour*

one of them was sent to the IVRI, it was discovered that the hyena was infected with rabies. It was possible that while preying on rabid village dogs, the leopard may have been contaminated with the disease in the same way as the hyena in Sariska probably got infected while scavenging on the remains of a rabid kill.

DAULAT SINGH SHAKTAWAT

Facing page and above: Cremating the leopard

My suspicions were proved correct when we got the report from the IVRI. The mystifying leopard of Mishr Darra had not been 'possessed' by any evil spirit but had rabies, which explained the abnormal behaviour of the otherwise elusive and secretive cat.

THE UNSUNG HEROES OF RANTHAMBHORE

They are the true heroes, men who fought valiantly and often gave up their lives and livelihood for the protection of others. It is their memory that I salute, for, without their brave efforts, many a life would have been lost in the wild.

I have spent half of my service tenure in the Forest Department at the Ranthambhore Tiger Reserve. Yet, when I sit back and look at the Reserve today, I am simply amazed at the progress it has made. The credit for this achievement goes, to a large extent, to the continuous efforts of the entire staff members of the Department. Starting from the cattle guards and forest guards to the field directors and chief wildlife wardens, they have all strived during the past four decades to give the Reserve their best. The district administration of Sawai Madhopur, the police, local communities, various non-government organisations working here, wildlife enthusiasts across the world and people associated with tourism have also helped make it one of the best tiger reserves of the country. Among these, there were some who gave up their lives or suffered permanent disabilities in order to make the Reserve what it is today. It saddens me immensely when I see that neither the local communities nor the present forest staff know about these unsung heroes of Ranthambhore.

In 1973, when the Ranthambhore forest was selected as one of the first nine Tiger Reserves of India, some restrictions and regulations were imposed on forest resource extraction by the local people around the Park. Thereafter, in December 1980, a part of the Tiger Reserve was notified as the Ranthambhore National Park and a complete ban on various anthropogenic activities such as livestock grazing, tree cutting and lopping, mining and so on was enforced. Such stringent prohibition, however, led to an increase in the incidents of recurrent conflicts between the park management and the local communities. Several of these incidents turned into lethal episodes of bloodshed when some of the forest staff members lost their lives, while others became physically incapacitated.

T-18 at the Reserve: As a result of better management practices, the tiger numbers in Ranthambhore have gone up

DAULAT SINGH SHAKTAWAT

Violent conflicts persisted for a long time in Ranthambhore. Both the Central and the State Governments tried to reduce these clashes by initiating various developmental projects to minimise the rift between the park management and the local communities. Centrally sponsored schemes of village relocation for the forest dwelling communities helped them to rehabilitate to new surroundings. The relationship between the local communities and the park management improved significantly. As a result of better management practices, the tiger numbers in Ranthambhore went up, which helped the local tourism industry to develop. A lot of jobs were generated. While the growing number of tigers augmented the local economy of Ranthambhore with the continual growth of the tourism industry, man-animal conflict incidences also increased owing to the same reason.

There have been several incidents that have impacted Ranthambhore's history considerably. In 1981, the Field Director of the Ranthambhore National Park, Fateh Singh Rathore, was attacked by a crowd of 40 to 50 residents of Uliyana village who were illegally grazing their livestock in the Lakarda forest areas of the National Park. Rathore was on patrolling duty and he suffered severe injuries. His driver, Saiyad Mohammed, tried his best to save him and he, in turn, also got seriously injured. A year later, these two brave men were presented the Fred M Packard International Parks' Merit Award in New Delhi.

On 1 August 1985, a mob from Sherpur and Khilchipur villages attacked a forest team near Mishr Darra, who had been patrolling to prevent illegal grazing activities. The crowd charged at the team with weapons and a forester, Hari Singh, got seriously injured. He succumbed to his injuries in the Sawai Madhopur Hospital. I was then the Range Officer, along with YK Sahu, ACF. Both of us and several forest staff—Manohar Singh, Mahendra Singh, Kedar Prasad, Bhanwar Singh and Vikram Singh—were critically injured during that incident. We were all given a special certificate of appreciation and a cash reward by the Chief Wildlife Warden.

The majestic 36 Pillars Chhatri *inside the Tiger Reserve*

A glorious sunset
at the Aravalli hill ranges
in Ranthambhore

DAULAT SINGH SHAKTAWAT

Bhadya was an honest, brave tiger tracker and a hardworking game watcher. The tracking of animals during the monsoons becomes difficult and erratic, but you could always see Bhadya, armed with his long-handled axe and tracking kit, diligently going about his duty. I often saw Bhadya accompany Fateh Singh Rathore when the latter went patrolling. I realised that there had to be something very special about this non-assuming tiger tracker for Rathore to take him along with him all the time. Whenever I got an opportunity, I would also ask him to come with me on my tracking expeditions. He was a fearless and simple man who performed his duties with total dedication. From his vast repertoire of knowledge and first-hand experience, he gave me some important tiger/leopard tracking tips, which are extremely useful to me even today. Unfortunately, he died under mysterious circumstances in December 1991.

In April 1993, when a team of the forest department caught a few poachers and was bringing them in a government vehicle to the Sawai Madhopur headquarters, they were ambushed on the way by the accomplices of the nabbed criminals. Those people were armed with guns and other firearms and they opened fire at the team without any warning. Forester Ramgopal Puri and forest guard Kalyan Singh died on the spot, while the driver Devi Singh and home guard Raj Singh Gurjar were grievously injured.

*The last photograph of Sundari (T-17) before she
disappeared from the Park*

In November 1994, a team from the forest department was patrolling to prevent illegal grazing activities in the Bodal areas of the Ranthambhore Tiger Reserve, when they came upon a large herd of livestock. Somehow, they managed to push and lock the livestock in the cattle pond of the Bodal forest *chowki*. Upon receiving this information, a large number of people from the nearby villages attacked the forest *chowki*. Forester Parminder Singh and forest guard Badan Singh were seriously injured. In March 1998, in the Bodal area of Ranthambhore, on the Sawai Madhopur road, the staff of Bodal *chowki* was carrying out routine checking and patrolling to stop poaching and other illegal activities. Forest guard Sukhvir Singh saw a suspicious truck speeding along. He tried to stop it, when it slowed down, by grabbing the driver through the window. But the truck sped away, dragging Sukhvir Singh for some distance before dumping him on the road. Sukhvir Singh succumbed to his injuries.

In 2002, a joint patrolling team of the Police and Forest Departments went to thwart illegal grazing operations. On their way back to Sawai Madhopur with the offenders, an angry mob attacked them in village Uliyana. In that deadly attack, the Deputy Superintendent of Police, Prem Singh Chandrawat, was seriously wounded, along with others. Two years later, in August 2004, a forest team was operating to prevent illegal grazing in the Lambi forest area near Lakarda of the Tiger Reserve, when they were suddenly attacked by a mass of villagers who wanted to take away the offenders and the seized livestock. In that deadly attack, forest guard Phool Chand was so gravely wounded that he is now completely paralysed for life.

On 20 August 2010, a sub-adult male tiger killed a buffalo in the agricultural fields of the village Bhuri Pahari, at the periphery of the Ranthambhore Tiger Reserve. Thousands of people gathered at that spot and started pelting stones at the tiger. Forest Department officials and police personnel rushed to the spot. It appeared that chemical immobilisation was the only option for rescuing the tiger from that location. Though the situation at the site was not suitable, yet, I, along with foresters Hukum Chand and Tulsi Ram and forest guard Rajveer Singh, reached the spot to tranquillise the tiger. Continuous disturbance by the mob made the tiger jump on me. Today, I have 40 per cent physical disabilities with the permanent loss of sight in my right eye.

Ghishu Singh (extreme left) with the author (fourth from left), one month prior to his tragic death

On 25 October 2012, assistant forester Ghishu Singh was supervising forest road repairing work in the Kalapani-Sohan Kachchh areas under the Sawai Madhopur range of the Reserve. During foot patrolling, a male tiger T-24 (Ustad) unexpectedly pounced at him and killed him. Thereafter, the tiger dragged his dead body to the nearby dense undergrowth. When the Forest Department teams arrived at the spot, it took a lot of effort to reach the dead body as the aggressive tiger was very possessive about his kill. The forest personnel somehow managed to acquire the body from that location.

In the evening of 8 May 2015, routine patrolling duty was going on by a Forest Department team with forester Hukum Chand, forest guard Rampal Mali and other staff members near the areas between the booking tent barrier and the Mishr Darra gate. Ustad attacked Mali from a forest trail near the main road next to Atal Sagar. With a mighty blow, the tiger killed him instantly. The accompanying forest team somehow managed to free the dead body from the tiger.

I have tried my best to recount all the major incidents of the unsung heroes who have contributed to the conservation of the Ranthambhore Tiger Reserve. These incidents are based on my recollections or collected from the official records of the Forest Department of Ranthambhore. Needless to say, there could well be some omissions or errors, but none of them are intentional. I realise that there may be many others who have contributed significantly towards the conservation of this last remaining semi-arid tiger gene pool in India. I express my deepest gratitude to all these heroes. It is their sacrifices that make us proud.

RAJESH GUPTA

EPILOGUE

Among all the tiger reserves in India, Ranthambhore is possibly the most talked about wildlife habitat in the north-western part of the country. Is this because of its rugged beauty or its easy accessibility from Jaipur and Delhi? Without taking away from these two positives, I think what attracts wildlife lovers from all over the world is the 'great sighting' of the tiger here.

$\mathcal{C}$lear visibility in the scrub dry deciduous forests and the unabashed nature of the tigers draw people to the Ranthambhore Tiger Reserve. Anyone who comes here seems to get hooked and cannot help but visit the Park again. For it is, ultimately, the inhabitants of the Reserve, the Big Cats, that are its biggest draw. Among them was Machhli (T-16), who was the heart-throb of millions of tiger lovers for over two decades; she was also the single-most photographed tigress of the Indian forests. Dozens of documentaries have been made on her and these continue to enchant all, even when she is no longer around. In her lifespan of 20 years, she had four litters, giving birth to nine cubs. Two of these cubs were sent to the Sariska Tiger Reserve to repopulate the area.

Machhli got her celebrity status after killing a crocodile, measuring three metres, at the Rajbagh Lake. She became quite a proficient crocodile hunter after that. She was an extraordinary bold tigress who strode among parked tourist vehicles with her cubs without any hesitation. Machhli has the rare distinction of being awarded the Lifetime Achievement Award by the Tour Operators For Tigers (TOFT), which is a unique international campaign advocating and supporting responsible tourism as a way to save the

DAULAT SINGH SHAKTAWAT

Machhli's daughter,
Sundari (T-17), in a
playful mood with a hare

tiger. She also has a Facebook page dedicated to her. In spite of having lost all her canines, Machhli managed to survive in the wild for five years. On 18 August 2016, she finally succumbed to old age, thereby ending the saga of the 'Lady of the Lake'.

Tigress Sundari (T-17) was the daughter of Machhli from her last litter. Just as bold and daring as her mother, she dislodged Machhli from the Rajbagh Lake and took over the territory; she dominated Tourist Zones 2, 3, 4 and 5 and became a great hit with visitors. Sundari mated with

*Machhli, seen behind the
author's vehicle*

T-28 and gave birth to a litter of three cubs. When the cubs were about 11 months old, this beautiful tigress suddenly disappeared and was never seen again.

An aggressive, pugnacious male, T-25 earned himself the epithet Zalim or tyrant. But, contrary to his nature, he surprised the forest staff when he raised T-5's cubs, who were only four months old when their mother died. Wildlifers bemoaned the death of the tigress as much as the loss of the cubs because death seemed inevitable for such small cubs without

Noor (T-39) with the cubs
from her third litter

Zalim (T-25) surprised the forest staff when he raised T-5's cubs, who were only four months old when their mother died

BALENDU SINGH

the presence of their mother. Their father, Zalim, stepped in and nurtured the little ones, bringing them food and later giving them lessons about surviving in the wild.

Ranthambhore has seen many other bold and exceptional tigers. It is not possible to enumerate them all here or talk about their exploits. Star Male (T-28), Kumbha (T-34) and Noor (T-39) are some who have successfully littered and raised to adulthood the magnificent tigers of Ranthambhore. It is to this splendid breed that I dedicate my last words, literally. The Epilogue of this book is a testimony to the greatness of some individual tigers and others who remain forever in the minds of many, having created a lasting impression by their presence. Their strength, agility and power are indeed legendary. Sometimes, it takes only a glimpse to begin a narrative, a love story as it were, with the national animal of India, the tiger.

APPENDIX ONE

Fauna of the
Ranthambhore Tiger Reserve

Class Pisces

Bita	*Lahio rohita*
Catla	*Catla catla*
Greyei	*Chhana marulion*
Lanchi	*Walago auto*
Mahseer	*Tortor spp.*
Mirgal	*Circhinus mrigala*
Roho	*Labio rohita*
Savank	*Chhana punctatus*
Seenghari	*Mystus seenghala*

Class Amphibia

Common Frog	*Rana tigerina*
Common Indian Toad	*Bufo melanostictus*

Class Reptilia

Banded Krait	*Bungarus fasciatus*
Cobra	*Naja naja*
Common Krait	*Bungarus caeruleus*
Desert Monitor Lizard	*Varanus griseus*
Freshwater or Swamp Crocodile	*Crocodylus palustris*
Ganga Soft-shelled Turtle	*Trionyz gan*
Indian Chameleon	*Chameleon zeylanicus*
Indian Python	*Python molurus*
North Indian Flap-shelled Turtle	*Lissemys punctata*
Rat Snake	*Ptyas mucosus*
Russell's Viper	*Pipera russelli*
Saw-scaled Viper	*Echis carinatus*

Class Aves

Alexandrine Parakeet	*Psiattacula eupatria*
Ashy-crowned Finch-Lark	*Eremopterix grisea*
Ashy Wren Warbler	*Prinia socialis*
Bank Myna	*Acridotheres ginginianus*
Bar-headed Goose	*Anser omdocis*
Barn Owl	*Tyto alba*
Baya	*Ploceus philippinus*
Bay-backed Shrike	*Ianius vittatus*
Bittern	*Botaurus stekkaris*
Black-backed Woodpecker	*Chrysocolaptes fesativus*
Black-bellied Tern	*Sterna acuticauda*
Black-breasted Quail	*Coturnix coromandelica*
Black-capped Kingfisher	*Halcyon pileata*
Black-crowned Finch-Lark	*Eremopterix nigriceps affinis*
Black Drongo	*Dicrurus adsimilis*
Black Eagle	*Ictinaetus malyensis perniger*

Black-necked Stork	*Ephippiorhynchus asiaticus*
Black-headed Oriole	*Oriolus xanthornus*
Black Partridge	*Francolinus francolinus*
Black Red Stork	*Phoenicurus ochruros*
Black Stork	*Ciconia nigra*
Black-tailed Godwit	*Limosa limosa*
Black-throated Thrush	*Turdus ruficollis*
Black-throated Weaver Bird	*Ploceus benghalensis*
Black-winged Kite	*lanus caeruleus*
Black-winged Stilt	*Himantopus himantopus*
Blossom-headed Parakeet	*Psittacula cyanocephala*
Blue Rock Pigeon	*Columba livia*
Blue Rock Thrush	*Minticola solitarius*
Blue Throat	*Erthacus svecicus*
Bylth's Reed Warbler	*Acrocephalus dumetorum*
Bonelit's Hawk-Eagle	*Hieraaetus fassciatus fasciatus*
Brahminy Kite	*Haliastur indus*
Brahminy Myna	*Sturnus pagodarum*
Brown Crake	*Amauronis akool akool*
Brown Fish Owl	*Bubo zeylonesis*
Brown Flycatcher	*Muscicapa latirosrtis.*
Brown-headed Kingfisher	*Pelargopsis capensis*
Brown Rock Chat	*Cercomelafusca*
Bronze-winged Jacana	*Metopidusindicus*
Bush Lark	*Mirafra assumica*
Cattle Egret	*Babulcusibis*
Changeable Howl-Eagle	*Spizaetus cirhatus*
Chiffchaff	*Phylloscopus collybita*
Collared Bush Chat	*Saxicola torquata*
Collared Owl	*Otus bakkamocna*

Collared Sand Martin	*Riparia riparia*
Common Babbler	*Turdoides caulatus*
Common Grey Hornbill	*Tockus birostris*
Common Hawk-Cuckoo	*Cuculus varius*
Common Nightjar	*Caprimulgas asiaaticus*
Common Pochard	*Aythya ferina*
Common Redshank	*Tringa totanus*
Common Rosefinch	*Carpodaucs erythrinus*
Common Sandpiper	*Tringa hypoleucos*
Common Snipe	*Gallinago gallinago*
Common Starling	*Strunus vulgaris*
Common Teal	*Anas crecca*
Coot	*Fulica atra*
Cotton Teal	*Nettapus coromandelianus*
Crag Martin	*Hirunda rupestris*
Crested Bunting	*Melophus lathami*
Crested Hawk Eagle	*Spizaetus cirrhotus cirrhatus*
Crested Honey Buzzard	*Pernis ptilorhynchus*
Crested Lark	*Galerida cristata*
Crested Serpent Eagle	*Spilornis cheela*
Crimson-breasted Barbet	*Megalaima heamarcephala*
Crow Pheasant	*Centropus sinensis*
Cuckoo	*Cuculas canorus*
Darter	*Anhinga rufa*
Desert Wheatear	*Oenanthe deserti*
Dusky Crag Martin	*Hirundo concolor*
Dusky Horned Owl	*Bubo coromandus*
Dusky Leaf Warbler	*Phylloscopus fuscatus*
Egyptian Vulture	*Neophron percnopterus*
Falcated Teal	*Anas falcata*
Fire-capped Tit	*Cephalopyrus flaimiceps*
Frankin's Nightjar	*Caprimulgus affinis monticola*

Frankin's Wren-Warbler	*Pronia hodgsoni*
Gadwall	*Anas strepera*
Gargancy Teal	*Anas qverquedula*
Glossy Ibis	*Plegodis falcinellus*
Golden-backed Woodpecker	*Dinopium benghalenus*
Golden Oriole	*Oriolus orilus*
Great Spotted Eagle	*Aquila clanga*
Great Horned Owl	*Bubo virginianus*
Great Reed Warbler	*Acrocephalus stentoreus*
Grayish Leaf Warbler	*Phylloscopus trochiloides*
Green Pigeon	*Terron phoenicoptera*
Greenshank	*Tringa nebuaria*
Green Sandpiper	*Tringa ochropus*
Grey-headed Flycatcher	*Culicicapa ceylonesis*
Grey-headed Myna	*Sturnus malabaricus*
Grey-headed Yellow Wagtail	*Motacilla flava thunbergi*
Grey Heron	*Ardea cinerea*
Greylag Goose	*Anser anser*
Grey-necked Bunting	*Emberiza bunchanani*
Grey Partridge	*Francolinus pondicerinus*
Grey Quail	*Coturnix coturnix*
Grey Shrike	*Lanius excubitor*
Grey Tit	*Parus major*
Grey Wagtail	*Motacilla easpica*
Gull-billed Tern	*Gelochelidon nilotics*
Hoope	*Upupa epops*
House Crow	*Corvus splendens*
House Sparrow	*Passer domesticus*
House Swallow	*Hirundo tahitiea*
House Swift	*Apus affinis*
Indian Chiff Swallow	*Hirundo fluvicola*
Indian Common Myna	*Acridotheres tristis*
Indian Course	*Cursorius coromandelica*
Indian Desert Finch-Lark	*Ammomanes deseri phoenicuroides*
Indian Griffon Vulture	*Gyps fulvus fulvescens*
Indian Myna	*Acridotheres tristis*
Indian Moorhen	*Gallinula chloropus*
Indian Robin	*Saxicoloides fulicata*
Indian Roller	*Coracias benghalensis*
Indian Shag	*Phalacrocorax fuscicollis*
Indian Tree Pipit	*Anthus hodgsoni*
Indian Wren-Warbler	*Prinia subflava*
Iore	*Aegithina tiphia*
Jungle Babbler	*Turdoides striatus*
Jungle Bush Quail	*Perdicula asiatica*
Jungle Crow	*Corvus macrorhyncos*
Jungle Nightjar	*Caprinulgus indicus*
Kashmir Roller	*Coracias garrulus semenowi*
Kashmir Plover	*Charadrius alexandrinus*
Kestrel	*Falco biarmicus*
King Vulture	*Sarcogyps calvus*
Koel	*Eudynomys scolopcea*
Lagger Falcon	*Falco biarmicus*
Lapwing	*Vanellus vanellus*
Large Cormorant	*Phalacrocorax carbo*
Large Cuckoo-shrike	*Coracina novahollandiae*
Large Desert Lark	*Alaemon alaudipes doriae*
Large Egret	*Ardea alba*
Large Green Barbet	*Megalaima zeylanica*
Large Grey Babbler	*Turdoides malcolmi*
Large-pied Wagtail	*Motacilla moderaspatensis*

Large White-rumped Swift	*Apus pacuficus pacificus*
Lesser Spotted Eagle	*Aquila pomarina hastata*
Lesser Whire Throat	*Sylvia curruca*
Lesser Whistling Teal	*Endorcygna javanica*
Little Brown Dove	*Streptopelia senegalensis*
Little Cormorant	*Phalacrocorax niger*
Little Egret	*Egretta grazetta*
Little Grebe	*Podiceps ruficollis*
Little Green Heron	*Butorides striatus javanicus*
Little Ringed Plover	*Charadrius dubius*
Long Billed Vulture	*Gyps indicus*
Long Legged Buzzard	*Buteo runfinus runfinus*
Magpie-Robin	*Copsychus saularis*
Marsh Harrier	*Circus aeruginosus*
Marshall's Iora	*Aegithina nigrolutea*
Marsh Sandpiper	*Tringa stagnatilis*
Median Egret	*Egretta intermedia*
Montagu's Harrier	*Circus pygargus*
Nakta or Comb Duck	*Sarkidiornis melanotos*
Olivaceous Leaf Warbler	*Phylloscopus griseolus*
Open Billed Stork	*Anastomus oscitans*
Orange-headed Ground Thrush	*Zoothera citrina*
Osprey	*Pandion haliaetus*
Painted Partridge	*Francolinus pictus*
Painted Sandgrouse	*Pterocles indicus*
Painted Snipe	*Rostratula benghalensis*
Painted Spurfowl	*Galloperdix lunudata*
Painted Stork	*Mycetria parvus*
Palm Swift	*Cypsiurus parvus*
Paradise Flycatcher	*Terp siphone paradisi*
Pariha Kite	*Milvus migrans govinda*

Peafowl	*Pavo cristatus*
Pheasant-tailed Jacana	*Hydrophasianus chirurgus*
Pied Bush Chat	*Saxicola caprata*
Pied Crested Cuckoo	*Clamator jacobinus*
Pied Kingfisher	*Ceryle rudis*
Pied Myna	*Strunus contra*
Pintail	*Anas acuta*
Pitta	*Pitta brachyura*
Plain Leaf Warbler	*Phylloscopus neglectus*
Pond Heron	*Ardeola grayi*
Purple Heron	*Ardea purpurea*
Purple Moorhen	*Galinula Porphyrio*
Purple Sunbird	*Nectarinia asiatica*
Pygmy Woodpecker	*Picoides nanus*
Red-breasted Flycatcher	*Muscieapa parna*
Red-crested Pochard	*Netta rufina*
Red-headed Bunting	*Emberiza brunicers*
Red-headed Merlin	*Falco chicquera*
Red-legged Falcon	*Falco vespertinus*
Red-rumped Swallow	*Hirundo daurica*
Red Spurfowl	*Galloperdix spadicea*
Red Turtle Cove	*Streptopelia tranquebarica*
Red-vented Bulbul	*Pycnonotus cafer*
Red-wattled Lapwing	*Vancellus indicus*
Red-whiskered Bulbul	*Pycnonotus jocosus*
Ring Dove	*Streptopelia decaocto*
River Tern	*Sterna aurantia*
Rock Bunting	*Emberizacia spp.*
Rock Bush Quail	*Perdicula argoondah*
Rose-ringed Parakeet	*Psittacula krameri*
Rosy Starling	*Strunus roseus*
Ruddy Sheldrake	*Tadorna feruginea*

Ruff and Reeve	*Philomachus pugnax*	Tawany Eagle	*Aquila rapax*
Rufous-backed Shrike	*Lanius schach erythronotus*	Temminck's Stint	*Calidris temminckii*
Rufous-bellied Babbler	*Dumetia hyperythra*	Tickell's Blue Flycatcher	*Muscicapa tickeliiae*
Rufous-fronted Wren-Warbler	*Prinia buchanani*	Tickell's Leaf Warbler	*Phylloscopus affinis*
Rufous-tailed Finch-Lark	*Ammomanes phoencurus*	Tree Pie	*Dendrocitta vegabunda*
Rufous Turtle Dove	*Streptopelia orientals*	Tree Pipit	*Anthus trivialis*
Sarus Crane	*Grus antigone*	Tufted Duck	*Anyhya fullgula*
Scarlet Minivet	*Pericrocotus flammeus*	Verditer Flycatcher	*Muscicapa thalassia*
Scopes Owl	*Otus scops*	Whiskered Tern	*Childenias hybrida*
Shaheen Falcon	*Falco peregrinus*	White-backed Vulture	*Gyps bengalenois*
Shikra	*Accipiter badius*	White-bellied Drongo	*Dicrurus ceerulescens*
Short-toed Eagle	*Circuetus gallicus*	White-breasted Kingfisher	*Halcyon snyrmensis*
Short-toed Lark	*Calandrella cinerea*	White-breasted Waterhen	*Amaurornis phoenicurus*
Shoveller	*Anas clypeata*	White-browed Fantail Flycatcher	*Rhipdiura aureola*
Singing Bush Lark	*Mirafrs javanica cantillans*	White-capped Bunting	*Emberisa stewarti*
Sirkeer Cuckoo	*Taccocua leschenaultii*	White-cheeked Bulbul	*Pycnonotus leucogenys*
Small Blue Kingfisher	*Alcedo atthis*	White-eye	*Zosterops palpebrosus*
Small Green Bee-eater	*Merups orientalis*	White-eyed Buzzard Eagle	*Butastur teesa*
Small Minivet	*Pericrocotus cinnamomeus*	White-eyed Pochard	*Aythya nyroca*
Small Skylark	*Alaudagugula*	White-headed Yellow Wagtail	*Motacilla flava leucocephala*
Smoky Willow Warbler	*Phylloscopus fuligiventer*	White Ibis	*Threskiornis aethiopica*
Sparrow Hawk	*Accipiter nisus*	White-necked Stork	*Ciconia episoopus*
Spoon Bill	*Platalea leucorodia*	White Stork	*Ciconia ciconia*
Spotted Dove	*Streptopelia chinensis*	White-throated Munia	*Lonchura malabarica*
Spotted Munia	*Lonchura punctulata*	White Wagtail	*Motacilla alba*
Spotted Owlet	*Athene brama*	Wigeon	*Anas penelope*
Spotted Redshank	*Tringa erythropus*	Wire-tailed Swallow	*Hirundo smithii*
Spur-winged Lapwing	*Vanellus spoinosus*	Wood Sandpiper	*Tringa glareola*
Stone Curlew	*Burhinus oedicnemus*	Wood Shrike	*Teprodornis pondicerianus*
Streaked Fantail Warbler	*Chisticola juncidis*	Wryneck	*Jynx torquilla*
Streaked Weaver Bird	*Ploceus menyar*		
Tailor Bird	*Orthotomus sutotius*		

Yellow-browed Leaf Warbler	*Phylloscopus inornatus*
Yellow-cheeked Tit	*Machlolophus spilonotus*
Yellow-eyed Babbler	*Chrysomma sinense*
Yellow-fronted Pied Woodpecker	*Picoides mahrattensis mahrattensis*
Yellow-headed Wagtail	*Motacilla citreola*
Yellow-legged Button Quail	*Turnix tanki*
Yellow-throated Sparrow	*Petronia xanthrocollis*
Yellow-wattled Lapwing	*Vanellus malabaricus*

CLASS MAMMALIA

Blue Bull or Nilgai	*Boselaphus tragocamelus*
Caracal	*Felis caracal*
Common Langur or Hanuman Langur	*Presbytis entellus*
Common Mongoose	*Herpestes auropuncfatus*
Common Palm Civet or Toddy Cat	*Paradoxurus hermaphroditus*
Common Yellow Bat	*Scotophilus heathis*
Desert Cat	*Felis libyca*
Five-striped Palm Squirrel	*Funambulus pennanti*
House Mouse	*Mus musculus*

House Rat	*Rattus rattus*
Indian False Vampire	*Megaderma lyra*
Indian Flying Fox	*Pteropus gigateus*
Indian Fox	*Vulpex bengalensis*
Indian Gazelle or Chinkara	*Gazella bennettii*
Indian Gerbille	*Tetera indica*
Indina Mole-Rat	*Bandicota bengalensis*
Indian Porcupine	*Hystrix indica*
Indian Wild Boar	*Sus scrofa*
Jungle Cat	*Felis chaus*
Leopard	*Panthera pardus*
Long-eared Hedgehog	*Hemiechinus auritus*
Ratel	*Mellivora capensis*
Rufous-tailed Hare	*Lepes nigricollis rufieaudatus*
Sambar	*Cervus uncolor*
Sloth Bear	*Melursus ursinus*
Small India Mongoose	*Nerpestes edwardsi*
Small Indian Civet	*Viverricula indica*
Spotted Deer or Chital	*Axis axis*
Stripped Hyaena	*Hyaene hyaena*
Tiger	*Panthera tigris*

APPENDIX TWO

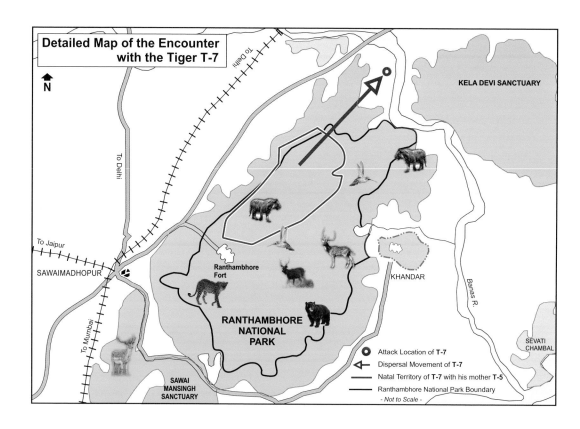

Detailed Map of the Encounter with the Tiger T-7

N

To Delhi

To Delhi

KELA DEVI SANCTUARY

To Jaipur

SAWAIMADHOPUR

Ranthambhore Fort

KHANDAR

Banas R.

To Mumbai

RANTHAMBHORE NATIONAL PARK

SEVATI CHAMBAL

SAWAI MANSINGH SANCTUARY

Attack Location of **T-7**

Dispersal Movement of **T-7**

Natal Territory of **T-7** with his mother **T-5**

Ranthambhore National Park Boundary

- Not to Scale -

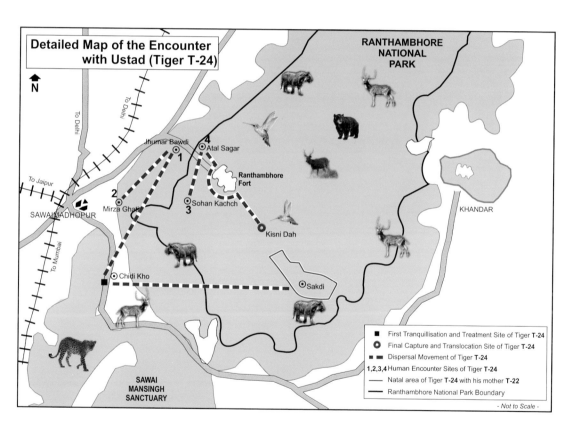

Detailed Map of the Encounter with Ustad (Tiger T-24)

N

RANTHAMBHORE NATIONAL PARK

To Delhi
To Delhi
To Jaipur
SAWAIMADHOPUR
To Mumbai

Jhumar Bawdi
1
4 Atal Sagar
Ranthambhore Fort
2 Mirza Ghati
3 Sohan Kachch
Kisni Dah
KHANDAR
Chidi Kho
Sakdi

SAWAI MANSINGH SANCTUARY

■ First Tranquillisation and Treatment Site of Tiger T-24
◎ Final Capture and Translocation Site of Tiger T-24
■ ■ Dispersal Movement of Tiger T-24
1,2,3,4 Human Encounter Sites of Tiger T-24
— Natal area of Tiger T-24 with his mother T-22
— Ranthambhore National Park Boundary

- Not to Scale -

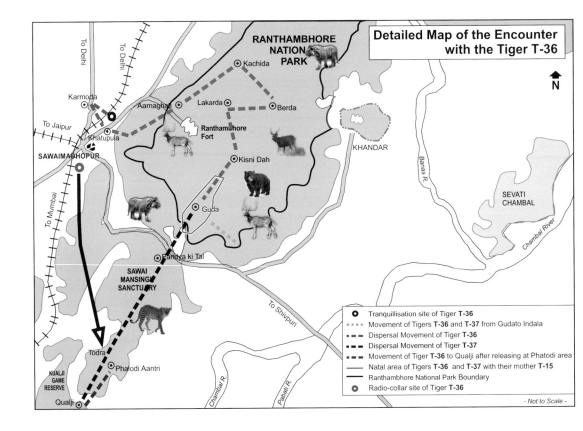

Detailed Map of the Encounter with the Tiger T-36

RANTHAMBHORE NATIONAL PARK

N

To Delhi
To Delhi
To Jaipur
To Mumbai

Karmoda
Kachida
Aamaghati
Lakarda
Berda
Khatupula
Ranthambhore Fort
SAWAIMADHOPUR
Kisni Dah
KHANDAR
Banas R.
SEVATI CHAMBAL
Chambal River
Guda
Pandya ki Tal
SAWAI MANSINGH SANCTUARY
To Shivpuri
Todra
Phalodi Aantri
KUALJI GAME RESERVE
Qualji
Chambal R.
Pabati R.

⊙ Tranquillisation site of Tiger T-36
▪▪▪▪ Movement of Tigers T-36 and T-37 from Gudato Indala
▪▪▪ Dispersal Movement of Tiger T-36
▪▪▪ Dispersal Movement of Tiger T-37
▪▪▪ Movement of Tiger T-36 to Qualji after releasing at Phatodi area
— Natal area of Tigers T-36 and T-37 with their mother T-15
— Ranthambhore National Park Boundary
⊙ Radio-collar site of Tiger T-36

- Not to Scale -

ACKNOWLEDGEMENTS

I consider myself extremely fortunate to have had the opportunity to work under two stalwarts in the field of wildlife conservation in India—Padma Shri Kailash Sankhala and Fateh Singh Rathore. They were my foremost gurus from whom I have learnt a lot. Among other things, the two mantras that they gave me were to visit the forest every day and to observe and understand the signs and happenings in the jungle. Sankhala Sahib also taught me to observe carefully and thereafter to document, daily, whatever I had seen. These are the mantras that I have been following till date and they have worked really well for me.

I would like to thank SR Yadav, Dr Dharmendra Khandal, Sunny Patil, Aditya Singh, Dinesh Verma Durrani, Bholu Abrar Khan, Hemraj Meena, Dhirendra Ghodha, MD Parashar, Peter Prem Chakravarthi and the Forest Department for giving me their photographs for this book. I am grateful to the Keoladeo National Park and the Rajasthan Forest Department for allowing me to use the photograph of the tiger being tranquillised.

I am indebted to my seniors, colleagues and subordinates—people within and outside the Department who have enriched my journey by their presence and exchange of knowledge. I have tried my best to remember them all but, in case I have omitted anyone, it is inadvertent and I apologise for it. My special thanks to Kailash Sankhala, Fateh Singh Rathore, Jai Singh, Paney Singh, VD Sharma, RS Bhandari, S Ahmad, Santanu Kumar,

RG Soni, UM Sahay, AS Brar, P Som Shekhar, GV Reddy, Govindsagar Bhardwaj, Rajesh Gupta, RS Shekhawat, Anup KR, KL Saini, JS Nathawat, Tejveer Singh, Sunayan Sharma, YK Sahu, Rahul Bhatnagar, BM Sharma, RK Kherwa, SR Yadav, Mukesh Saini, Mahendra Sharma, Sudarshan Sharma, Nand Lal Prajapat, Rangalal, Valmik Thapar, Dr K Shankar, Dr PK Malik, Dr Paraag Nigam, Dr Rajeev Garg, Vikram Singh Chouhan, Girraj Singh Kushwah, Akhil Chandra, Dinesh Verma Durrani, Sanjay Casshyap, Zuzar Tinwalla, Pushp Jain, Harshvardhan, Suraj Ziddi, Dharmendra Khandl, Rajpal Singh, Raj Singh, Bittu Sehgal, Jaisal Singh, Goverdhan Singh Rathore, Balendu Singh, Gopaldutt Pandey, Bholu Abrar Khan, Mahipal Singh, Devendra Ratnawat, S Nallamuthu, Anis Andheriya, Adeet Ghosh, JS Hada, Uday Ram, Sanjeev Sharma, Mangal Singh Rathore, RS Kala, Mohal Lal Garg, Narayan Singh Naruka. MD Parashar, CP Sharma, Sunil C Shah, Hansraj Bairwa, Kailash Navrang, Narayan Kumawat, Shyamji, Ramprasad, Devi Sahay, Hiralal, Dharm Singh, Papu Singh, Rama Shanker, Suresh, Yogesh, Manohar Singh, Mahendra Singh, Saeed Mohammad, Rajveer Singh, Hukam Chand, Tulshi Ram, Ranjeet Singh, Abhey Singh, Phool Chand, Mohan Singh, Satpal, Shivraj Singh, Manoj Kumar Sharma, Bhenrow Ram, Purshotam, Jagdish Prasad Jat, all naturalists and the tourist drivers at the Park. I am grateful to Virender Kumar for preparing the maps for this book.

I would also like to express my heartfelt gratitude to Ashok Gehlot, Ex-Chief Minister of Rajasthan; RN Mehrotra, Head of Forestry Force (Retd.) and Ex-Chief Wildlife Warden, Rajasthan Forest Department; and Ravi Singh, Secretary General, WWF India, for the immense help and cooperation extended during my hospitalisation and prolonged treatment after the unforgettable incident that took place on 20 August 2010.